THE LITT...
Orchids

Geneviève Carbone
Yves Delange
Jean-Claude Gachet
Mireille Lemercier

Flammarion

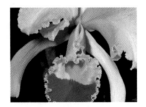

From Confucius' China to ancient Greece, from the Amazonian rainforests to the shores of the Indian Ocean, from the Aztec ruler Montezuma to the wealthiest Europeans of the nineteenth century, the orchid has excited the senses and inspired imaginations. What mysteries does the orchid hold for us today?

One in twelve flowering plants on this planet is an orchid. Lady's slippers sprout on several continents. Mexican vanilla is cultivated as a commercial crop thousands of miles from Mexico. How have human activities, from commerce to science, pastimes to passions, influenced the evolution and the appreciation of the orchid?

Orchid flowers are captivating and their methods of propagation are fascinating. How do they attract insects to help them reproduce?

Orientation p. 6

The alphabetical entries have been classified according to the following categories. The categories are indicated with a small colored rectangle.

■ Botany:
Species,
Reproduction,
Anatomy and
Symbiosis

■ Orchid Growing:
Techniques
and care

■ History:
Commerce, arts, and
symbolism

The Story of Orchids p. 10

The Story of the Orchid provides a detailed overview of the themes and information provided in the alphabetical entries.

Alphabetical Guide p. 28

The entries tell what you need to know to enter the universe of orchids. They are enriched with detailed discussion of the main varieties of orchids, historical information, clarification of botanical complexities, and growing tips.

I. ORCHID HUNTERS

A. To Die for a Flower

The worldwide expansion of maritime exploration and trade enabled Europeans to discover orchids, among other treasures. Botanists and other scientists soon joined these voyages, often risking life and limb in their efforts to catalogue the world's natural wonders.

B. A Challenge to Science

From the very beginnings, botanists have been gathering and classifying orchids, as well as analyzing their uses. Now they must also work to protect them against the harmful effects of human activities.

C. Cultivation

It is not easy to grow orchids outside of their natural habitats. Extensive research has been devoted to understanding their reproductive processes and to developing new varieties for home growth and commercial cultivation.

II. A FLORAL TRILOGY

A. The Flower

An orchid flower's structure and unique biological organization is as fascinating as its singular form and sumptuous colors.

- *Beans and the Vanilla Plant*
- *Flower Parts*
- *Flowers and Fruit*
- *In Vitro Germination*
- *Labellum*
- *Meristem*
- *Roots*
- *Sexual Reproduction*
- *Spontaneous Propagation*
- *Temperate Zone Orchids*

B. The Insect

While some orchids are capable of self-pollination, most require the help of particular insects to reproduce. Orchids lure them in with visual, olfactory, tactile, and anatomical tricks.

- *Evolving Together*
- *Insects*
- *Labellum*
- *Pollination: A Bag of Tricks*
- *Sexual Reproduction*

C. The Fungus

Tiny orchid seeds cannot germinate without a fungus. The discovery of the symbiotic relationship between orchids and fungi was a decisive stage in the understanding of orchid biology.

- *Bernard, Noël*
- *In Vitro Germination*
- *Seedlings*
- *Seeds*
- *A Symbiotic Relationship*

III. FROM THE WILDS TO THE LIVING ROOM

A. Thousands of Species

The *Orchidiceae* family is one of the largest and most diverse in the plant kingdom, and flourishes throughout vast range of climates and regions.

- *The Americas*
- *Classification*
- *Common Names*
- *Dioscorides*
- *Epiphytes*
- *Geographic Distribution*
- *Lady's Slipper*
- *Temperate Zone Orchids*
- *Terrestrial*
- *Vanilla History*
- *The Vanilla Trade*

B. Forests to Greenhouses

Of many varieties of orchids growing in the wild, only tropical orchids have long been taken from their natural environments and cultivated in greenhouses.

- *Arrival in Europe*
- *Botanical Gardens*
- *Canopies*
- *Common Names*
- *Chatsworth*
- *Dioscorides*
- *Epiphyte*
- *Geographic Distribution*
- *Greenhouses*
- *Habitat*
- *Lady's Slipper*
- *Orchid Hunters*
- *Terrestrial*
- *Vanilla History*

C. Cultivation, Commerce, and Home Growing

Learning to cultivate orchids has been a trial-by-error process, but at last their methods of reproduction have been mastered. Today, botanical research facilitates large-scale cultivation and has greatly improved the availability of adaptable and beautiful plants for home growing.

- *Acclimation*
- *Compost*
- *Disease*
- *Fertilizing*
- *Foodstuffs*
- *In Vitro Germination*
- *Light*
- *Moisture*
- *Repotting*
- *Salep*
- *Seedlings*
- *Seeds*
- *Stakes*
- *Temperature*
- *Outdoor Growing*
- *Propagation*
- *The Vanilla Trade*
- *Ventilation*
- *Watering*

IV. ORCHID MANIA

A. Passion for Collecting

"Orchid fever" spread throughout Europe during the eighteenth century. While collectors' zealous enthusiasm initially led to the endangerment of numerous orchid species, it also ultimately brought about a greater understanding of botany.

- ■ *Bernard, Noël*
- ■ *Buying Orchids*
- ▨ *Chatsworth*
- ■ *CITES*
- ▨ *Collecting, Then and Now*
- ■ *Conservation*
- ■ *Endangered Species*
- ■ *Greenhouses*
- ▨ *Orchid Hunters*
- ■ *Societies*
- ▨ *Traveling Botanists*

B. The Orchid as Status Symbol

Driven by their passion, European orchid enthusiasts built verandas and greenhouses in which to display their prized plants. Their seductive beauty led to a popular craze, with the most lovely blooms commanding exorbitant prices.

- ▨ *Botanical Gardens*
- ▨ *Chatsworth*
- ▨ *Collecting, Then and Now*
- ■ *Greenhouses*
- ▨ *Symbolism: Beauty, Art, and Potency*

C. Exotic Fantasies

It is not only the rarity and the price of the orchid which seduces. Its beauty—fascinating and troubling—casts its spell too, influencing artists and writers around the globe.

- ▨ *Literature*
- ▨ *Love and Death*
- ▨ *Symbolism: Beauty, Art, and Potency*

THE STORY OF ORCHIDS

Orchids are one of the largest of all plant families. They flourish worldwide, in both hemispheres, blooming from the equator to the poles. The range of their shapes, sizes, and colors is tremendous, but orchids all share a very particular flower structure and idiosyncratic reproductive systems. The orchid's special biological makeup makes it dependant on insects* for pollination,* and on specific fungi for nutrients.

Like the rose, the orchid has long held a privileged place in man's heart. Honored in the Far East for thousands of years, its praises were sung in the sixth century by Confucius (551–479 B.C.E.), father of Chinese philosophy. In the ancient and medieval world, the orchid was prized for its medicinal uses. It wasn't until the seventeenth century, however, that tropical orchids first made their way to Europe,* as part of the many exotic treasures brought back by explorers. Ever since, Western botanists have ceaselessly studied, catalogued, cultivated, and experimented with this plant which made—and still makes—them dream, amateurs and professional horticulturalists alike.

I. Orchid Hunters
A. To Die for a Flower

As part of European expansionism in the seventeenth through nineteenth centuries, traveling botanists* and intrepid orchid hunters* set out on expeditions in search of the new. Whether from scientific fervor, greed, or a thirst for adventure, this special breed of botanical bounty seekers routinely risked life and limb for the sake of flowers. Among them were Joseph Banks, later the honorary director of the new Royal Botanic Gardens at Kew, and John Gibson, whose daring exploits brought back hundreds of species to his patron, the duke of Devonshire, making his estate at Chatsworth* home to the foremost orchid collection of its time.

B. A Challenge to Science

Adventuresome botanists and plant hunters often fell prey to tropical diseases, danger on the high seas, or other misfortunes. Alexander von Humboldt, * and the others who returned triumphant, helped build extensive orchid collections in the West. Today, outstanding ones may be found English, American, Dutch, Swiss, French, and Australian botanical gardens.

Gallé workshop, *Study of Cypripedium for glass inlay work,* 1902–1903. Pencil, ink, and watercolor. Musée d'Orsay, Paris.

The list of orchids specialists is long and still growing. These experts must grapple with the ever-increasing problem of endangered* or extinct orchid species, largely the result of the industrial and demographic expansion which has overtaken the natural habitats* of many orchids. The almost irresistible temptation to pick wild orchids has also taken its toll.

Measures have been passed to help conserve* and protect orchids: the Convention on International Trade in Endangered Species of Wild Flora and Fauna (CITES)* was drawn up in

Washington D.C. in 1973. Today about a hundred and fifty countries subscribe to this treaty.

C. Cultivation

Wild orchids are astonishingly diverse and beautiful. These species are the core of botanical garden collections, * to the delight of the public. Unfortunately, they are not well suited for commercialization. The flowers blossom too briefly, are too fragile, and cannot be transported easily. They may also be

Antoine Phelippeaux, *The Expeditions of Cook and La Perouse*, c. 1799. Engraving. National Library of Australia, Canberra.

Anonymous, *Charles Darwin with Charles Lyell and Joseph Hooker* mid-1800s. Oil on canvas. Royal College of Surgeons, London.

either too large or too small to be of practical interest to houseplant growers. Since methods of seed germination have been developed, orchid varieties and crossbreeds can be adapted to suit the houseplant market.

Plant crossbreeding normally involves fertilizing the flower of one species with another species from the same genus. But orchids lend themselves to crosses between different genera as well. There are two-genus crosses, such as *Laeliocattleya* from *Laelia* and *Cattleya*, and three-genus crosses such as *Sophrolaeliocattleya* from *Sophronitis* plus *Laelia*, and *Cattleya*. Orchid hybrids* have also been created from up to five genera and multiple species, allowing specialists great freedom to select and blend outstanding characteristics. While the process can set genetic tradition on its head, the results can be breathtakingly gorgeous.

II. A Floral Trilogy
A. The Flower

Orchids love threesomes. In fact for them it takes three, not two, to tango: flower,* insect,* and fungus. The orchid flower's structure itself is triple, with three sepals, three petals, three stamens, and sometimes three carpels. In most ornamental orchids the monotonous structure is relieved by the fact that each of the three sepals and other parts of the bloom and fruit can be so different in color, and even texture and shape, that only a trained botanist might see the congruities. One of the three petals, the labellum,* is almost always very different from the other two in shape, size, and coloring. The distinctiveness of the labellum plays a part in attracting insects for pollination.* Sometimes the labellum can have a nectar-producing spur.

In orchids, the organs of sexual reproduction* are likewise highly distinctive. Instead of producing pollen in powder form, the male stamens make pollinia, sticky pollen masses. Another feature unique to orchids is the *gynostem,* joining male and female organs; orchid reproduction is thus highly complex, and dependant on a third party—the insect.

B. The Insect

A limited number of orchids self-pollinate. But the majority, in a process detailed at length by Charles Darwin,* need the help of an insect to propagate. Different orchids require specific insects: *Vanilla* (a genus of the orchid family) pollinates naturally only in the Americas,* with the aid of the little melipone bee. Outside of its natural habitat, or with no melipone bees available, vanilla must be artificially pollinated.* Orchids with

Lycaste skinneri, Central America

long labella* or nectar spurs, such as the *Angraecum* indigenous to Madagascar, need the help of a butterfly or moth whose proboscis is a compatible length. Orchids and insects often have symbiotic relationships: the pseudobulbs of some Mexican *Schomburgkia*, for example, shelter ants who excrete the nitrogen necessary for reproduction into the plant. This kind of alliance between orchid and insect species help the evolution of both in turn.*

C. The Fungus

The third party in the triangle is another organism: fungus. Orchids rely on internal fungi to provide them with nutrients. Before this fact was discovered by the French botanist Noël Bernard* in 1899, orchids could not be grown from seed by humans. In the earliest stages of germination, fungus plays a major role in orchid growth.

The orchid and fungus develop a symbiotic relationship* in which each element provides something the other is missing on its own. In some cases, *Rhizoctonia* or mycorrhizal fungi continue to live among the roots after the orchid has matured. In others, the symbiotic relationship with fungus lasts throughout the orchid's entire life cycle. Orchids such as *Neottia nidus-avis,* for example, rely on the fungus to meet the needs that photosynthesis fills for most other plants.

Moth on *Ophrys insectifera,* France

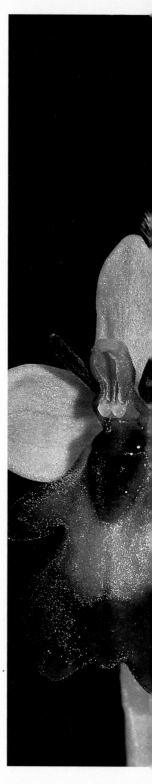

16

III. From the Wilds to the Living Room
A. Thousands of Species

The two largest plant families in nature are the *Compositae,* which numbers thirteen hundred genera and twenty-one thousand species, and the *Orchidacea,* with about seven hundred and fifty genera and nearly thirty thousand species. In addition, orchids grow over an extensive range of territory, from a southern latitude of fifty-six degrees to a northern one of sixty-eight degrees. Density varies greatly with climate. The humid tropics have by far the most orchids—for instance, there are three thousand species of orchids growing in Colombia alone, while New Caledonia and Madagascar host some two hundred species. Many orchids thrive in restricted habitats,* but others are found in a wide range of locations. *Vanilla,** for example, is found in the Americas,* Africa, Madagascar, the Comoros, and Polynesia. It can thrive at sea level or atop a mountain, and withstand prolonged drought and cold spells.

Orchis.
Plate from
François Pierre
Chaumeton's
Flore médicale.
Paris, 1814-18.

Facing page:
*Himantoglossum
hircinum,*
France

Although orchids first appeared two hundred million years ago during the Jurassic era, they display signs of more recent evolution. In temperate zones and much of Australia, the predominant orchid species are terrestrial,* meaning they grow in the ground. But most tropical orchids, and therefore most orchid species in the world, are epiphytes,* or plants that grow on other plants. This is the result of evolutionary adaptation to forest and jungle habitats. Orchids may also be lithophytic, growing on rocks instead of plants, and adapted to dry conditions.

B. Forests to Greenhouses

Many orchids are protected species or difficult to grow. These species are mainly the concern of botanists. People who grow orchids in greenhouses concentrate their efforts on tropical or subtropical epiphytic* varieties. The majority of these orchids come from Asia, Indonesia, and the Americas.* Asian varieties include *Dendrobium, Aerides, Coelogyne, Cybidium, Vanda, Paphiopedilum, Phalaenopsis,* and *Cirrhopetalum.* Those from Central and South America include the less common *Stanhopea* and *Gongora* genera, *Laelia, Cattleya, Odontoglossum* and *Miltonia,* and *Epidendrum* and *Brassia* some of whose species derive from as far north as Florida. African orchids that are frequently grown in greenhouses include *Angreacum, Bulbophylum,* as well as the delicate *Disa.*

Most orchids like humus-rich potting compounds for their roots.* Air and soil should be kept humid and moist,* but allowed to dry periodically during the plants' dormant phases.

Orchid greenhouses are kept cool, warm, or hot, according to the orchids they house. Very few pure botanical species are found in greenhouses these days. Commercial orchids sold by growers and florists are generally cultivated varieties (known as cultivars) which may or may not resemble the plants collected by botanists in tropical forests.

C. Cultivation, Commerce, and Home Growing

Before discovering the fungi essential to orchid growth, the only known ways to propagate orchids were by division and cutting techniques. This made for exorbitant prices and slow growing. Once the first *Rhizoctonia* fungi were identified and propagated in a laboratory,

Renanthera monachica, the Phillipines

21

Vanda hybrids   it became possible to grow orchids from seedlings, by means of sexual reproduction.* Since the 1970s, meristem* in vitro cultivation has been used. The technique induces orchid seeds* to germinate in sterilized flasks of agar, producing plants big enough for transplanting in a matter of weeks. It takes from

two to seven years for these plants to be mature enough to become available for sale at nurseries.

In recent decades, imported orchids grown in the tropics have come to comprise a significant share of the market. But the number of species available is restricted compared with the

23

wealth of fascinating hybrids* developed by professional breeding specialists. These growers offer an ever-changing range of orchid options.

VI. ORCHID MANIA
A. Passion for Collecting

Among nineteenth-century orchid lovers, the collector's passion at times reached pathological heights. Fortunes are known to have been plundered, and lives risked, for the sake of a single flower.

Taking hold around 1850, the orchid collecting* craze raged in England, France, Belgium, Germany, and Russia. Coming as they did from tropical regions, and subjected to the ordeal

Kew Gardens, London, c. 1900

of maritime shipping, the orchids so ardently sought by the collectors more often than not perished en route. Those that survived the journey didn't fare much better: only a few months after its introduction in England, *Cattleya labiata* var. *automnalis* was so popular as to become an endangered species.

One of the rare nineteenth-century orchid collectors who managed to keep a level head was an American, Edward Sprague Rand. A graduate of Harvard, he practiced law but his true passion was floriculture. He wrote and edited numerous works on flowers, including *The Complete Manuel of Orchid Culture* (1876), and left his extensive floral collection to his alma mater.

B. The Orchid as Status Symbol

The great botanical gardens established in the nineteenth century, such as Kew Gardens in London, included lavish tropical greenhouses* full of outstanding orchid collections.* The upper classes quickly sought to imitate these at home. Orchids became

fashionable status symbols,* and certain species fetched outlandish prices. Orchid specialist Désiré Bois at the Museum of Paris and author of Orchids, the Growers' Manual, quoted the following prices: 600 francs for an *Angraecum eburneum* in 1830, 2,525 francs for an *Aerides schroderae* in 1855 and 4,500 francs

Laeliocattleya hybrid, Tangerine Chitchat

(ten times the annual salary of a chambermaid) for a *Vanda sanderiana*. Empress Eugenie, the consort of Napoleon III, was not alone in paying tremendous sums for her orchids, though her *Cattleya triannae,* bought for 18,000 francs in 1867, topped the records.

C. Exotic Fantasies

Orchids seem to inspire more fantasy than all other flowers put together. In the Far East, orchids have had a religious function and for thousands of years have appeared in myths, legends, and works of art. In regions of the Indian Ocean and Africa, orchids have been used as aphrodisiacs, and in Central America they served in religious ceremonies, including ritual sacrifices. At an International Orchid Conference, the portrait photographer Takashi Kijima recently presented his new collection of photographs of orchids. According to him, these flowers "have always been appreciated for their feminine forms. Their association with eroticism is greater than with any other flower."

From the moment Europeans became aware of their intriguing shapes, mesmerizing perfumes and amazing beauty at

Hokusai (1760–1849), *Yellow Orchids*. Print. Musée Guimet, Paris.

the end of the seventeenth century, orchid cultivation* and collection* became almost obsessive. Since then, they have been a continuing source of inspiration for artists: they were a favorite of the Pre-Raphaelite arts movement in Great Britain in the second half of the nineteenth century, and have been praised by writers as various as Oscar Wilde, Henry David Thoreau, Marcel Proust, H. G. Wells, and Rex Stout.

With their astonishing, even shocking, beauty, fascinating habitats, and innumerable species and secrets, orchids provide any plant lover with endless possibilities not only for hours of happy gardening, but also for hours of reverie.

Yves Delange

■ Acclimation

Acclimation is the process of becoming accustomed to a new habitat* or environment. If an orchid's growing conditions are gradually modified to acclimate it to a new location, the plant can make a healthy transition. It was not until the middle of the nineteenth century that well-meaning attempts to grow orchids in overheated conditions were rethought. Before that point, misconceptions about tropical climates led to the loss of thousands of plants. Now that reproducing orchids has become easier, it is pointless, and often illegal, to remove them from their native surroundings. In their countries of origin, orchids are not always sold under ideal conditions. Specimens may be offered for sale too soon after being collected. They may be damaged, too old, or contain an insufficient quantity of pseudobulbs. It can take years for plants that have survived such ordeals to recover and thrive. If you are buying* a plant far from home, be sure to keep it dry during the trip back, and up until the point when you repot* it. Seedlings sold in sealed containers acclimate best. Orchid species removed from temperate habitats* are no less finicky. It is extremely important to get all of the plants roots, or else most species will die. In addition, acclimating a plant to a location even a couple of yards away may prove fatal to it. Some indispensable element, such as a symbiotic* fungus may be lacking. ML

■ The Americas

The fragrant fruit of *Vanilla* orchids was valued by native American populations for its medicinal and therapeutic qualities. Vanilla* played a major role in Aztec daily life and economics. Their records indicate that from the reign of Izcoatl (1427–1440) onward, the Totonacapans on the eastern coast of Mexico gathered and cultivated wild pods, paying their taxes with vanilla.

The Spanish conquistadors landed in the Americas a few decades after Columbus in hope of conquering the New World. Along with gold they found a wealth of unexpected botanical treasures, including

tobacco, cacao, and orchids. It is said that when the conquistador Hernán Cortés arrived in Mexico in 1519, the ruler Montezuma greeted him with a drink made of cacao beans and chocolate, flavored with vanilla. Montezuma is reported to have drunk this heavenly beverage a minimum of fifty times a day, each time served from a little pot supposedly of pure gold.

The Spanish brought vanilla pods back to Europe to display along with other "Indian oddities." Vanilla was soon in high demand to flavor chocolate and tobacco, and botanists sought ways of growing it in both

Auguste Garneray, *Interior of the Malmaison Greenhouse* (detail), 1812. Watercolor. Musée national du château de Malmaison, France.

Title page from Karl Ludwig Blume's *The Most Remarkable Orchids of the Indian Archipelago and Japan.* Amsterdam, 1858.

"Spaniards Arriving in Tlaxcala," *Durán Codex,* c. 1579–81. Biblioteca Nacional, Madrid.

Europe and New World. But it was not until Joseph Neumann* discovered artificial pollination* in 1830 that *Vanilla* would yield fruit on new ground. Soon after, vanilla plantations were set up in Jamaica, Florida, Australia, New Zealand, and tropical parts of Asia, and Africa. GC

Arrival in Europe

The first orchid to arrive in Europe probably came to the Netherlands, as it is known that a *Brassavola nodosa* from Curaçao was grown by Casper Fagel as soon as the early 1680s. The first orchid to actually flower in Europe was the Englishman Sir Charles Wager's *Bletia purpurea*. The historic bloom appeared in 1732, on an orchid acquired in the Bahamas a year earlier. By the mid-eighteenth century, tropical orchids were being cultivated in France, Holland, Russia and North America.

Botanical experimentation, knowledge, and techniques advanced with the ever-increasing number of orchids being imported to Europe from Asia and South America.

The Genera and Species of Orchidaceous Plants, a masterwork of orchid classification by the English botanist John Lindley, appeared in 1830. Lindley was Assistant Secretary at the Royal Horticultural Society, then known as the Horticultural Society of London. His many publications and presentations did much to expand orchid knowledge in England. Kew Gardens soon acquired Lindley's collection. A companion piece to Lindleys's *Genera and Species* was Franz Bauer's *Illustrations of Orchidaceaous Plants,* which catalogues almost all orchids known in the 1830s. By 1840 some three thousand species were already classified. During the next decade, *Orchid Grower's Manual,* probably the first instructive books on orchids, was written by the Irishman J. C. Lyons,. and published at his own expense. In 1852, Lyons's work was furthered by the appearance of Benjamin Williams's important *The Orchid Grower's Manual.* A little later, other landmark works were published by Jean Linden,in Belgium and Alfred Celestin, Cogniaux in France. YD

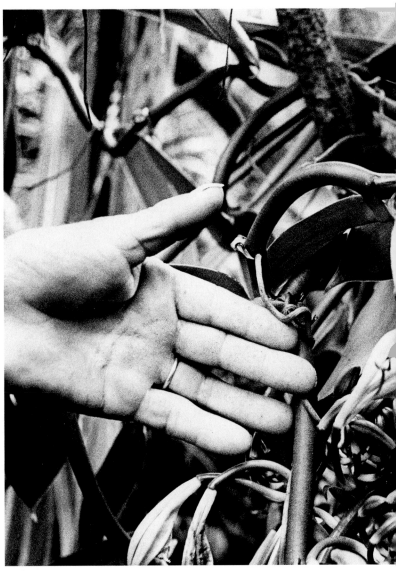

Artificial pollination, which must be used when no insects* are available to do the job, is fairly simple.

An orchid's sexual organs are grouped at the tip of its column, which is comprised of the stamens, or male parts, and the female part, known as the style. Just below are the pollinia—clumps of pollen grains normally transported and deposited by insects on another flower's stigma, the sticky area designed to receive the pollen. The pollinia are protected by the anther cap, which guards against self-fertilization. If this cap is raised and the pollinia are lowered, a plant will fertilize itself. Credit for the discovery and implementation of this

straightforward technique is a matter of debate; the date of its first use is set somewhere between 1830 and 1840. The method is still used today, especially for growing vanilla.*

Cross pollination, or pollination between two different plants, can be done manually as well. Pollen grains are gathered with a pointed instrument such as a toothpick or knife tip, and placed on the stigma of another orchid. This type of pollination is used to create new hybrids,* and to propagate orchids, such as the *Paphiopedilum,* that do not respond to meristem* cultivation. ML

Artificial pollination of a vanilla flower in Réunion

33

■ Beans and the Vanilla Plant

There are a hundred and ten known species of *Vanilla*,* a genus of orchid in the *Epidendrum* family. Its natural habitat* extends between the twenty-seventh parallels, north and south, on the continents of Asia, Africa, and North America. Only about fifteen species produce edible fruit. Three of these which are commercially grown are *Vanilla planifola, Vanilla pompona,* and *Vanilla tahitensis.*

In botanical terms, the pods of vanilla plants are technically "capsules," the dry fruit of flowering plants that pop open upon maturity to spread their seeds.

Vanilla planifola pods are greenish yellow and are four to ten inches (10 to 25 cm) long with diameters of about half an inch (8 to 15 mm). *Vanilla tahitensis* pods measure about five inches (12 to 14 cm), and are half an inch (10 mm) wide. *Vanilla pompona* measures about four inches (10 to 12 cm) by about an inch (16 to 30 mm).

Vanilla plants produce their first blooms two or three years after planting. The flower clusters last only eight hours. Outside of their native regions they are pollinated* by hand. Seven to ten months later, pods reach maturity but give off no odor. The fruit must be prepared in order for the aroma to be released.

Vanilla plants in Réunion

Vanilla bean
pods, Polynesia

Left:
Vanilla pompona,
French Guyana

The large pods of *Vanilla planifola* (also known as *Vanilla fragrans* or as Mexican vanilla, after its place of origin) produce beans with the highest vanillin content. Their flavor is superior to that of the other two species. Mexican vanilla is now commercially grown mainly in Madagascar and Indonesia. The large, dark green creeping plant reaches lengths of 45 feet (15 m). It puts out aerial roots* to cling to whatever is nearby for support. Its leaves are big, oblong and pointed and its inflorescence is comprised of from six to thirty flowers. The short-lived, highly fragrant blossoms produce capsules after artificial or natural pollination.* GC

vegetative and underground portion of a fungus. His ensuing research determined that orchid germination requires cooperation between the fungus and the orchid plant. This is called mycorrhizal symbiosis or mycorrhizal association. Noël understood the symbiotic* relationship as an evolutionary process.

Following his *Research on Orchids* (1904), he published *Evolution in Symbiosis* (1909), which explains the interrelationship of two organisms. His discovery that the fungus enters the very cell wall of the orchid embryo turned out to be an essential starting point for the study of immunology.

Bernard, Noël

Noël Bernard (1874-1911) was indispensable in finally understanding orchid anatomy and the germination process. In 1899 he discovered seeds* of bird's nest orchids (*Neottia nidus-avis*) that had begun to sprout in the French forest of Fontainebleau. Bernard noted the presence of a mycelium, the

Noël Bernard
(1874–1911)

Samuel Wale, (d. 1786), *The Oxford Botanical Garden.* Pen and black ink with gray wash. Ashmolean Museum, Oxford.

Noël's techniques for producing symbiotic seedlings with *Rhisoctonia* remained the primary method of cultivated orchid germination until the 1970s, when meristem* propagation, invented in 1960, came into widespread use. YD

▌Botanical Gardens

Orchids are difficult to spot in the wild. Many of the species indigenous to North America and Europe have become rare. Today, the majority of orchids grow in tropical and subtropical areas, but even seeking them out in a natural habitat* such as Amazonian rain forests is no easy task, because they thrive in the high canopies* formed among treetops. The difficulty of seeing orchids in the wild makes the greenhouses* in botanical gardens a great boon for orchid lovers.

In keeping with a system developed in the nineteenth century, orchids are grown in different greenhouses according to their native climate: hot, temperate, or cold.

Botanical gardens are highly educational, for inquisitive visitors and botany students alike. They also play and important role in the establishment of guidelines and protection for endangered* plants. Exotic orchid collections* require costly equipment and maintenance. The fragility of certain species actually makes it impossible to allow routine public access to them. Because flowering is periodical, botanical gardens often set up special orchid exhibitions in season.

The two most important botanical gardens in the United States are the New York Botanical Garden in New York City and the Missouri Botanical Garden in St. Louis. In Canada, the botanical gardens of Ottawa, Montreal, and Toronto are justly famous, while the numerous botanical gardens of Europe, include the Royal Botanic Gardens (known as Kew Gardens) in London, and the Jardin des Plantes in Paris. YD

Facing page: *Phalaenopsis* being grown for sale, France

■ BUYING ORCHIDS

The exact number of orchid species in the world today is a matter of speculation. Kew Gardens, for example, has a record of about forty thousand registered species and hybrids,* but it is not all-inclusive. In addition, there are more than a hundred thousand hort icultural varieties. And there are, of course, orchids yet to be discovered....

In light of such overabundance, professional orchid suppliers tend to specialize, either in species or in regions. All international commerce in orchids is regulated by CITES,* and there are about ten thousand species available on the market. Half of them, such as *Bulbophyllum,* are small plants with brilliantly colored little flowers. Hybrids and showy flowering species are highly sought after. Rarity and beauty can drive up the cost of a hybrid. For non-collectors, there is a wide range of beautiful, reasonably priced orchids to choose from. Some of the more common are *Phalaenopsis, Paphiopedilum, Cymbidium, Cattleya, Miltonia, Oncidium, Dendrobium,* and their hybrids. Remembering the orchid's exact name can come in handy later for growing advice. ML

■ CANOPIES

Phanerogams, or flowering plants, will die without sufficient light.* Yet even though only minimal levels of light reach the lower levels of tropical forests, flower bearing orchids still thrive in these jungles. How is this so?

In such primeval forests, the treetops form a canopy whose upper surface is home to many sorts of insects and plants, including orchids. Before the use of meteorological balloon stations, studying these phenomena usually required either coming upon a freshly fallen tree, or a climb that endangered the scientist and vegetation alike.

Meteorological balloons were first used for preliminary studies of treetop canopies in 1977. This led to the creation of a photographic mosaic of forest canopies in Gabon, compiled in 1978. Soon after, the French botanist Francis Hallé landed upon the same treetop habitats* in the dirigible *Summit Raft*. Recently, botanical studies in Panama and Venezuela have used cranes with 300 foot (100 m) long gangways to explore the upper reaches of tropical forests. YD

Cattleya intermedia, var. aquini "Rose," Brazil

The *Summit Raft*, Guyana, 1986

Chatsworth

The story of the nineteenth-century mania for orchids is full of eccentric aristocrats and obsessed millionaires.

Foremost among them was William George Spencer Cavendish, the sixth duke of Devonshire. The liberal-minded duke might have pursued a life in politics, were it not for his deafness, which caused him to shun the public eye. Instead, he devoted his immense fortune to indulging his passion for drama and the arts, and to this day, the art collection at his estate, Chatsworth, is deemed one of the finest in the world.

Devonshire had little use for plants until his early forties, when he first saw a *Psychopsis papilio* in bloom. He was so taken with the orchid's astonishing beauty that in almost no time he became a ardent collector and even president of the Royal Horticultural Society. His outstanding orchid collection was largely the work of Joseph Paxton, a gardener most famous for designing the Crystal Palace for Great Exhibition of 1851. Together, he and Devonshire redesigned the duke's many gardens. At Chatsworth they constructed a greenhouse measuring 43,056 square feet (4000 square meters) and known as the Great Stove. They found a third member of their team in John Gibson, a fearless plant hunter.* At their behest, Gibson went to India, where he collected and brought back more than a hundred formerly unknown orchid species. The bounty of Gibson's expeditions, Paxton's planning, and Devonshire's wealth and enthusiasm made the orchid

Wild orchid plants being sold in Bangkok, Thailand

CITES

Human activity has decimated so many plant species that collective action is essential for the conservation* of those that remain. The international effort to halt the process of extinction began with Convention on International Trade in Endangered Species of Wild Flora and Fauna (CITES), signed in Washington in 1973 by 122 countries. Today, about 150 countries are signatories.

CITES rates vegetation on a three-tiered scale, depending upon the degree of rarity. For instance, many tropical and North American orchids, and all European species, are currently listed under Appendix I, the most endangered. It is illegal to collect, hold, sell, import, or export them without official authorization. The sale of cultivated orchids also requires a CITES certificate. For plants brought from one country to another, an international export permit from CITES is required. Seedlings in flasks have recently been exempted from many of the requirements, and a seller's certificate of exportation suffices for the transport for older plants between countries within the European community. ML

collection at Chatsworth the most famous in the world. A number of orchids are named after the dedicated duke. They include *Cymbidium devonianum, Dendrobium devonianum, Galeandrea devoniana,* and *Oncidium cavendhsiuanum.*

■ Classification

The vegetable kingdom is comprised of several branches and variously classified subkingdoms. These include Bacteria, Algae, Fungi, Lichen, Mosses, Ferns, and Spermatophytes. Spermatophytes, or "seed plants," are probably the most biologically advanced, and are the most common. They have leaves, and divide into two groups, gymnosperms and angiosperms. Gymnosperms are cone-bearers; the most common of which is the conifer. They have carpellary (exposed ovule-bearing) leaves which form into cones and produce seeds after fertilization. Angiosperms are flowering plants. Their flowers contain one or more ovaries which produce seeds upon pollination* and develop into fruit.

Angiosperms are divided into dicotyledonus and monocotyledonus plants. Dicotyledons have two cotyledons (seed leaves) per plant, while monocotyledons are characterized by having only one cotyledon, as well as narrow leaves with parallel veins. The flower parts of monocotyledons—sepals, petals, stamens, and carpels—are arranged in threes.

There are about fifty thousand species of monocotyledons, which include lilies, bananas, cattails, grasses (including cereals and bamboo), some palms, and orchids.

Orchids contain two orders, the

Apostasiacae and the *Orchidaceae.* Species may also be divided into sub-species, varieties, and forms. There are three genera and twenty-five species of *Apostasiacae,* endemic to the Indonesian-Malaysian archipelago. With more than seven hundred fifty genera and almost thirty thousand known species, *Orchidaceae* constitutes one of the largest families in the vegetable kingdom. Orchids are distinguishable from other monocotyledons by the morphology of their flower parts and their reproductive systems. JCG

Portrait of Carl Linnaeus, after Lorenz Pasch. Oil on canvas. Musée national du château de Versailles, France.

Édouard Dubufe, *Empress Eugenie* (detail), 1853. Musée national du château de Compiègne, France.

■ Collecting, Then and Now

Nineteenth-century orchid mania was a pastime for the rich. An extensive collection was a mark of high social standing and proof of considerable financial outlays.

William George Spencer Cavendish, duke of Devonshire, spent a fortune on acquiring plants, starting in the 1830s. With the soon-to-be-famous Joseph Paxton, he constructed an enormous greenhouse known on his estate, Chatsworth,* and dispatched John Gibson on orchid hunting* expeditions that successfully brought back about a hundred and fifty species.

In France, the empress Eugenie paid tremendous sums for orchids in her collection. This included a famous purchase of a *Cattleya triannae* for eighteen thousand francs at the Paris Exhibition of 1867.

Many extensive European orchid collections were established during this period, including the National Historic Museum of Natural History in Paris (1834), and Kew Gardens in London (1844). The most grandiose orchid greenhouse of all was built for Leopold II, in Laeken, near Brussels. Leopold was so passionate about his plant collection that he died in one of his greenhouses.

A great-nineteenth century American collector, Edward Sprague Rand, was a rare exception to this mania. The noted author of many floriculture texts, he left his precious collection to Harvard University.

Nowadays, orchid collecting is a more democratic affair. This is thanks to modern reproduction techniques, particularly meristem* multiplication. But why grow orchids in the first place? Whether a hybrid, cultivar, or rare species, people are completely captivated by the beauty and complexity of the flower, and fascinated by its reproductive techniques. ML

Cattleya trianae

■ Common Names

Long before Linnaeus established his system of plant nomenclature in the eighteenth century, people throughout the world called plants by their own inventive names and continue to do so to this day. These common or vernacular names differ from region to region, dialect to dialect, and language to language. Only the scientific plant names are international.

The common names of flowers tend to be highly evocative or imaginative. Because they effectively underline the differences among flowers in a group, these names have often been used by botanists in official descriptions of orchid species. For example, Linnaeus kept the Greek word *ophrys* (eyebrow) to designate the *Ophrys* genre, made up of about a hundred and fifty orchids native to Europe and Asia Minor. Rather than producing nectar, the *Ophrys* genre devised the evolutionary strategy of making themselves resemble female insects* to attract pollinators.* This in turn led to names describing their looks, such as *Ophrys apifera,* the bee ophrys, *Ophrys insectifera,* the insect ophrys and (with its shiny labellum) *Ophrys speculum,* the mirror ophrys. Such names can be an aid to memory. Even the word orchid itself comes from the Greek word *orchis,* meaning testicle. For reasons of visual similarity with the underground roots of some orchids, Linnaeus kept this word.

Because orchids are indigenous to all parts of the world, there is an endless variety of common names to designate orchids. Many Amazonian orchids are referred to locally as "monkey love potions." Examples from the northeastern United States include *Pogonia,* known as beard flowers, and *Arethusa,* known as swamp rose orchids. In European countries, *Spiranthes* orchids (known as ladies' tresses or pearl twists in America) are called Virgin Mary's braid. North American varieties of *Cypripedium acaule* are known internationally as moccasin orchids. YD

Ophrys insectifera (fly orchid), France

Orchis simia (monkey orchid), France

■ COMPOST

Early attempts at growing orchids consisted of placing plants in pots filled with thick mixtures of rotting wood and leaves, and then keeping these pots in heated sawdust. If the plants didn't die from having their roots stifled, the parts outside the soil soon died in the hot dry air of early European greenhouses.* Finally however, the epiphytic* character of many orchids was understood, and conditions were created that gave roots* and the rest of the plant access to needed ventilation* and moisture.*

Orchid-growing composts are now commercially available. They are made of various combinations of natural and synthetic materials. The most common materials are pine bark, fibrous peat, perlag, horticultural charcoal, polystyrene, rockwool, and Styrofoam. These may be blended in various combinations, and fibrous peat or leaves may be added. The choice of one type of compost or another is a matter of personal taste, experience, and the particular orchid in question. Some orchid growers favor rockwool alone, or in combination with polyurethane.

Mixtures of pine bark with polyurethane pieces and small quantities of peat are also available. These are sold in fine, medium and heavy grades. Which grade to use depends upon the kind of orchid to be grown. But all such mixtures have the advantage of allowing the roots breathing room while at the same time retaining moisture.* After two or three years, compost must be completely replaced, since it is subject to bacteria and decomposition. Rockwool, on the other hand, is an inert material, and usually lasts a good five years before it must be changed.

In tropical regions, local materials such as peanut husks and coconut palm tree fibers are used. However, whatever the compost material, the larger the grain the more frequently it will require watering.*

Some orchids hate compost. They happily attach their roots to cork, oak bark or other surfaces, with perhaps the lightest dusting of peat moss in some cases. Rockwool cut into flat surfaces is another orchid favorite. Roots grow through the material, seeking out moisture.

Other orchids thrive in baskets or openwork pots, which allow maximum air circulation (*Vanda*) or the freest passage for flowering stems to develop among the pseudobulbs and roots (*Stanhopea*). ML

Cymbidium hybrid

Phalaenopsis roots being cleaned

Make sure that the compost is spread between the roots during repotting

Composts with different granule sizes

■ CONSERVATION

Many orchids exist only in particular natural habitats,* sometimes in very narrowly defined conditions and localized areas. They often depend upon specific insect* species for their complex and idiosyncratic pollination.* In addition, orchids' epiphyitic roots* are highly fragile. If moved, they have difficulty surviving under new climatic conditions, and their vital relationships with native flora and fauna are destroyed. CITES* was devised to combat this problem, but its focus is primarily on controlling the international orchid trade.

In the days of the orchid hunters,* the search for novelty species and the difficulties of orchid propagation* placed many orchids in danger. Today, the main threats to orchids are destruction of local habitats and, to a lesser extent, over-collecting. When ninety-eight percent of the forests of Singapore were cleared, for example, almost all endemic orchids became extinct. Meanwhile, throughout North America, the natural habitats of indigenous lady's slippers* (*Cypripedium*) have been depleted, and several *Cypripedium* species are endangered and protected.
JCG

Bulbophyllum flaviflorum, Taiwan

Charles Darwin, 1868. Photograph by Julia Margaret Cameron, Stapleton Collection.

■ Darwin, Charles

Before the publication of Charles Darwin's *Origin of Species* in 1859, botanists were well aware of the morphological resemblance between many orchid and insect* species in temperate climates. But they still did not fully understand how pollination* worked.

Darwin (1809–1882) studied the interdependent evolution of orchids and their insect pollinators. When he read Herman Crüger's observations on two orchid genera, Darwin became extremely interested.

Crüger's account describes how the labellum (or lip) of the *Coryanthes* orchids fills with water from the flower's two horn-shaped organs. Crüger noted that after bees had wet their wings in this little "pool,"

they could not fly off, and had to pass through a narrow conduit within the flower, thereby brushing against and transporting pollen for fertilization. Crüger also detailed the particular characteristics of the *Catasetum* genus. When a bee alights on certain *Catasetum* flowers, an "antenna" within the flower vibrates, releasing a viscous pollen liquid onto the insect's back. The bee then carries the pollen from stamen to anther for pollination.

Crüger's findings inspired Darwin to conduct the research which led to his *On the Curious Contrivances by Which British and Foreign Orchids Are Fertilized by Insects* (1862). This work definitively established the role of insects in orchid reproduction. YD

Coryanthes macrantha. Detail of plate from Jean Linden's *Iconography of Orchids,* Brussels, 1860.

From Dioscorides' *Materia medica.* Seljuk manuscript, 1228. Topkapi Palace Library, Istanbul.

■ **Dioscorides**

Orchids attracted learned and botanical attention in the East long before they became objects of interest in the West. This is probably due to the quantity of flora in China and Japan. In any event, centuries before the common era, orchids were used for medicinal* purposes. *Bletilla* and *Dendrobium* orchids even had religious and ritual applications.

Greek philosopher Theophrastus (372–287 B.C.E.) wrote several botanical treaties and was apparently the first Western authority to discuss a group of plants which he calls *orchis,* (testicle in Greek), because of the shape of its tubers. Of all Greek naturalists Dioscorides (40–90 C.E.) was the most knowledgeable on the subject or orchids. Born in the first century C.E., Dioscorides was a physician and a soldier with a keen interest in botany. During Nero's reign, he wrote *De Materia medica,* an important five volume work. Dioscorides called the *Orchis italica* (also known as *Orchis longicruris*) by the name *priapiskos* (little satyr or little Priapus). This species is native to Crete, Greece, and Southern Europe up through Portugal. When the flowers bloom in spring, the fields full of these orchids appear to teem with battalions of miniature humans.

Discorides was responsible for the idea of resemblance or signatures, which held sway in Western medicine at least until the Renaissance. According to this theory, medicinal plants could cure ailments of human body they resemble. For example, the walnut was believed to cure problems of the brain, and the orchid was a prescribed for potency and fertility problems. YD

■ Disease

Under the right conditions orchids grow into vital and healthy plants, but they can nonetheless fall prey to pests or disease. The main threat comes from insects,* including aphids, mealy bugs, vine weevils and cockroaches, caterpillars, and red spider mites. Fungus, certain forms of bacteria and viruses can also endanger orchids. But if carefully chosen and closely tended to, an orchid can have a healthy, disease-free existence.

The orchid's worst and most insidious enemy is the red spider mite, as well as several species of false spider mites. These insects are difficult to wipe out and hard for the naked eye to detect. Their thin webs and tiny silver spots on the lower surface of leaves are the clearest evidence of these bugs' presence. Red spider mites like dry, hot, close air, so they can be averted by spraying orchids with water. Insecticides should be used with caution, and to treat one problem at a time, as mixing

chemical products can lead to counter-reactions.

Slugs and snails can do considerable damage to orchids outdoors. This can be combated by spreading anti-slug powder in the growing area, and keeping a close eye on the plants, Such pests can be manually removed if found.

Over-watering, poor ventilation,* improper repotting,* cold, direct sunlight on a wet leaf, or various other forms of

Black rot on *Cattleya* leaves

Red spider mite seen under a microscope

Facing page:
*Cypripedium
calceolus,* France

carelessness can leave orchids vulnerable to fungal or bacterial rotting. Water is often the culprit. The tips of monopodial orchids and young plants should never be left wet. Poor drainage can rot orchid roots,* especially if there is peat in the compost.* If rotting is suspected, cut down on watering.* A plant that has begun to rot should be dried out, and the affected parts severely pruned and treated with a fungicide.

Phalaenopsis that has been moved and exposed to new conditions may lose its buds.

Viral infections in orchids are spread by direct contact. There is no known treatment, but the damage is often only on the surface. A plant whose leaves are discolored by a virus can be kept if it continues to grow and flower normally. Pruning can keep the damage from spreading. Sterilize the pruning tools before and after use. ML

■ ENDANGERED SPECIES

Over the past century, industrialization, demographic change, and other factors have turned some orchids into endangered species exiled from their natural habitats.* Other orchids have been brought to the point of extinction by over-picking. This is the case with several species of lady's slipper.* In recent decades, national legislation and international conventions have moved to protect wildlife and flora. The Berne Convention of 1979 protects European wildlife, flora, and their habitats. The treaty known as CITES* (Convention on International Trade in Endangered Species of Wild Fauna and Flora) was drafted in 1973 and took effect in 1975. Today about a hundred and fifty countries have approved, accepted, or ratified this accord. It strictly regulates international commerce in all orchids in the interest of conservation.* Another approach to conservation consists in setting aside the habitats of endangered species as nature preserves. There are also some successful instances of reintroducing endangered plants into the wild after propagation* in a controlled setting. JCG

*Bulbophyllum
lobbi,* Southeast
Asia

■ Epiphyte

More than half of all orchid species live in the tropics or subtropics, and three quarters of these are epiphytes—plants that grow on other plants. Their name is taken directly from Greek: *epi* means upon, and *phyton* means plant. They are not parasitic; instead they use the plants upon which they grow only as a support, taking nothing from them. This is the result of the conditions in their native forest and jungle habitats.* Tropical vegetation rapidly consumes all available nourishment, leaving the jungle floor drained of nutrients. The thick layers of growth make it difficult for the sun to reach the lower levels. In response to these factors, orchids have evolved* to live in the sunnier canopies* far above.

Some epiphytes prefer growing along bark crevices, living off the accumulated organic debris. Others have thicker aerial roots* that are always ready to catch hold of a tree or any other available surface; *Vanda, Phalanopsis,* and *Cattleya* orchids are in this group. Still others, such as *Oncidium* and *Maxillaria,* put out fine roots attuned to capturing and synthesizing moisture.* Orchids that grow along rocks are known as lithophytes. ML

Vanda tricolor

Left:
Microcoelia guyoniana

Right:
Epidendrum,
Martinique

Xanthopan morgani praedicta moth gathering pollen from an *Angraecum sesquipedale*

■ EVOLVING TOGETHER

The pollination* of terrestrial* orchids involves a close interrelationship with specific insect* species. In fact, particular orchids and insects evolved together over time, to their mutual benefit.

Recent studies have shown that some orchid flowers imitate the size, shape, color, texture, and even the scent of female insects in order to attract pollen bearing males. With the help of evolution, orchids have made amazing chemical and morphological changes for improved reproduction, without altering their basic structure. Thus, in some locations the *Ophrys apifera*, which already duplicated the shape of indigenous bees, has developed the capacity to pollinate itself.

Nor are examples of orchids and insects evolving together limited to the pollination process. For instance, when ants colonize the pseudobulb cavities of *Schomburgkia*, the orchid profits from the nitrogen contained in the aphids' excrement. YD

■ FERTILIZING

In their natural habitats,* humidity and decomposing vegetation ensure that orchids receive all the nutrients they need. In orchid cultivation regular fertilizing is necessary because the compost used cannot equal this capacity. Synthetic and other commercial fertilizers contain a combination of nitrogen (N), phosphorus (P), and potassium (K). All-purpose fertilizer should be diluted; most orchids can only handle these products at about one third their strength. Liquid fertilizer, added during watering, is the easiest alternative. Organic matter such as guano, ashes, and dried blood can also be used, as long as they provide or are supplemented with sufficient quantities of N, P, and K. How much fertilization is needed depends on other aspects of an orchid's growing conditions.

Orchids growing in rootwool most be fertilized quite frequently to compensate for the absence of nutritious matter, while those grown in a pine bark based compost require greater additions of nitrogen because the bacteria that break down pine are also greedy for nitrogen. Increasing

the amount of potassium in summer helps promote blooming.

If you are growing orchids indoors at home, it is usually sufficient to fertilize them during the spring and summer growing seasons only. Greenhouse* orchids may call for either a sizeable cutback on fertilizing elements, or their complete suspension in winter. Orchids grown on cork slabs or in baskets can be spray-fertilized with a highly diluted solution. Most orchids from temperate* northern regions of Europe and North America don't need to be fertilized at all. Never fertilize a sick plant, a plant that is in the process of acclimatizing,* or one that is in a dormant phase.

Orchids really do need less fertilizing than other flowering plants. Too much fertilizer will harm them. Roots get burnt and plants die if there is too much mineral accumulation in the compost. To prevent this from happening, water just before fertilizing, and use less than the recommended dose. ML

Orchid farm, Chiang Mai Province, Thailand

■ FLOWER PARTS

Like human bodies, the orchid flower is bilaterally symmetrical. One half of the flower is the mirror image of the other. The flower is comprised of threes, with three sepals, three petals, three stamens, and three carpels. The sepals are the outer parts of the flower. The three sepals together are called the calyx, and in most flowers they are green and serve to protect the inner parts. In orchids they resemble petals. There are two lateral and one dorsal sepal.

a: peduncle; b: labellum; c: stigma
d: apex of column; e: pollinia; f: lateral sepals
g: column; h: petals; i: dorsal sepal
j: viscidium; k: stalk; l: viscidium

The petals are located within the calyx. The central petal, known as the labellum differs from the other two. It sometimes has a spur that produces nectar. The labellum starts out growing from the back side of the flower and points upward. As it blossoms, the flower turns a hundred and eighty degrees, and the labellum rotates to the bottom. In a few species, though, this rotation either doesn't happen at all, or goes full circle, so the labellum remains at the top. This is the case for *Epipogium, Hammarbya, Liparis,* and *Nigritella.*

Two of the three stamens are infertile staminodes, and may be underdeveloped and have no pollen. The third stamen forms the male organ, or anther. The anther consists of two chambers which each hold one or two pollinia. Pollinia are masses of pollen grains clumped together. The pollinia are attached to a sticky gland, the viscidium, by a stalk. This whole pollen structure, called the pollinarium, is carried from one flower to another in pollination.*

The male and female parts are joined in the column. Two of the three stigma are fertile and fully functional, and they are fused together. The third stigma, known as the anther cap, is sterile. It keeps the anther's two chambers separate from the two fertile stigma, thereby preventing self-fertilization. As is often the case with orchids, there are some variations. A popular species which has two fertile stamens and three fertile stigmas is the lady's slipper,* *Cypripedium calceolus.* JCG

■ Flowers and Fruit

In autumn, some European orchids varieties (such as *Ophrys*) produce a rosette of leaves that then lasts through the winter. The most precocious orchids can bloom in January, while Mediterranean orchid varieties flower in March and April. The North American *Cypripedium* blooms in late spring or early summer, and some *Spiranthus* varieties bloom in autumn.

Under favorable climatic conditions, orchids will flower every year. Some autagamous orchids, those capable of self-pollination, will blossom under ground. This may be the case with *Neottia, Corallorhiza,* and *Epipogium.*

After blooming, if pollination* occurs, the ovary swells to produce the fruit, a capsule with three valves which dries upon maturity and releases tiny seeds.* Not all healthy seeds will make it through the stages of germination and growth.

An orchid's flowering cycle may last from a couple of weeks to several months, depending on the species. During the rest of the year, the plant makes its underground preparations for the next flowering cycle. JCG

Foodstuffs

While orchids may seem to be most appreciated for the way they look or smell, this has not always been the case. In regions of Central America, the Indian Ocean, and Oceania they have been important crops, with their subterranean portions used for food.

In Madagascar, Australia, and Tasmania colonists called the tubers of *Gastrodia sesamoides* "native potatoes." And like tulip bulbs, orchid tubers were recommended for eating in early modern Europe.

Different orchids have also been used for therapeutic purposes. On the islands of Madagascar, Mauritius, and Réunion, the leaves of *Angraecum fragrans* are dried and drunk as herbal tea, sometimes in combination with other tea leaves. Throughout the Mediterranean, the Middle East, and parts of the Indian subcontinent, *Orchis* tubers are boiled and reduced to a powder to produce salep* for beverages and sweets. Until the sixteenth century, vanilla* was known solely to certain Central American cultures, where it was an important part of their daily life. It was cultivated in the hot coastal lowlands, and used along with pepper as an ingredient in preparing chocolate. GC

Encyclia vitellina of Mexico and Guatemala

■ GEOGRAPHICAL DISTRIBUTION

With more than seven hundred and fifty genera and about thirty thousand species, the orchid family is one of the largest in the entire vegetable kingdom. Orchids are indigenous to every part of the globe except for the extreme north and south poles. Asia and South America are particularly plentiful in orchids. Many natural habitats* abound with diversified genera and species—a notable example is Madagascar.

The richness and variety of Asian orchids, including those in Indonesia, is astounding. *Cymbidium* grows in an area extending throughout China, the Himalayas, Korea, and Japan. Nine hundred species of *Dendrobium* flower in Malaysia, India, China, Japan, and the Philippines, as well as Australia and New Zealand. *Paphiopedilum* and *Phalaenopsis*, both favorites for producing hybrids,* thrive throughout India and the Philippines. Another major genus, *Vanda,* is indigenous from India and Taiwan to Austrailia.

Orchids are extremely abundant in Central and South America. There are hundreds of species of the memorable *Odontoglossum* (orchids with tooth-like protuberances on their labella), mainly growing to the west of the Andes. And there are sixty-five species of *Cattleya* native to the region, not to mention the large number of crossings with other local genres, such as *Brassavola, Epidendrum* and *Laelia.* These spontaneous hybrids have yielded some of the most breathtaking orchid color combinations. *Epidendrum* orchids range from the Carolinas to Argentina. The current count is up to about a thousand species.

In addition to lady's slippers,* or moccasin flower, some of the most common orchids in North America include *Spiranthes,* which are known as ladies' tresses or pearl twists; *Arethusa* (wild pinks, also known as swamp rose orchids); *Limodrum* or grass pink, which grows in meadows and swamps; *Pogonia,* or beard flowers; *Blephariglottis,* or fringe orchids; and various species of *Liparis* and *Listera* known as twayblades. Several species of *Corallorhiza,* or coral root, and *Neottia nidus-avis,* known as bird's nest orchid, can also be found, and the greenfly *Epidendrum* is native to the southeast.

Though Africa abounds in many other botanical riches, most of its orchids are rather fragile and difficult to grow. African *Angraecum, Ansellia, Eulophia,* and *Disa* are exceptionally beautiful.

There are a few hundred species of terrestrial orchids in Europe and the Mediterranean region, of which *Ophrys* is the most extraordinary. YD

Cattleya velutina,
South America

■ Greenhouses

When the rage for orchids hit Europe in the nineteenth century, collectors* immediately realized that greenhouses were needed to provide optimal growing conditions. At first greenhouses were a luxury for the very wealthy. But miniature greenhouses were soon mass-produced, making them more affordable for orchid lovers of modest means.

Orchid greenhouses provide plants with sheltered heat, ventilation,* watering,* and shade during the summer. All of these functions can be automated. Automation can also ensure constant monitoring to guard against overheating or frost.

The ideal direction for an orchid greenhouse is facing east-west. It should be in an unshaded area whose light is not blocked by a neighboring building. It is best for a greenhouse to be at least eight by ten feet (9 m²), as it is difficult to regulate the temperature* in a greenhouse of smaller dimensions. Minimum nighttime temperature in a cold greenhouse should be 50° F (10° C), which allows for the wintering of orchids from colder climates (*Pleione, Bletilla*), and permits orchids to rest before flowering, as needed with certain *Dendrobium (D. kingianum, D. delicatum)*, as well as *Odontoglossum,* and *Cymbidium.*

Hot greenhouse, Marcel Lecoufle growers, France

Right:
Epiphytes in a Brazilian Virgin Forest. Plate from Paul Emile de Puydt's *Orchids,* 1880.

Warm greenhouses reproduce a subtropical climate. The nocturnal temperature should be kept at 55 to 58° F (13 to 15° C), and daytime temperature should be maintained at about 75° F (24° C). These greenhouses are ideal for *Cattleya, Miltonia, Paphiopedilum,* and hybrid orchids.

Hot greenhouses simulate a tropical habitat.* Temperatures should be about 60° F (16° C) at night, and 80° F (27° C) during the day. Proper moisture* levels are essential; so is excellent ventilation.* Some of the loveliest orchids, including *Calanthe, Phalaenopsis* and *Vanda* flourish in these conditions.

A number of orchids also grow well outside the greenhouse. They can get adequate light, heat, and humidity in an apartment or house. Place them close to an east or west facing window, supplement humidity by placing orchid pots on pebbles in a tray of water, and remember that lower night temperatures are necessary for good growth. ML

■ **Habitat**

Natural habitats are technically known as biotopes. A biotope is the combination of physical and chemical factors, such as sunlight, temperature, humidity, hygrometry, and mineral composition, in which a particular living thing prospers. When a species flourishes somewhere it is said to be endemic to that place.

Most orchids are endemic to inter-tropical regions with heavy rainfall all year round. These are the orchids most readily available for buying,* and most amenable to greenhouse* conditions. Problems cultivating such orchids can result from misunderstanding their habitats—many orchid varieties grow solely in particular, or even extreme, biotopical conditions.

For example, some grow only on rocks alongside *Bromeliacea,* others only among epiphytic* cacti. Some botanical gardens* have xerophytic (arid zone) orchids, such as *Sarcanthus*

recurvus. This plant lives on steep and rocky slopes in Cambodia. Its large, overhanging aerial parts resemble those of lush African *Crassulaceae*. In Madagascar, *Vanilla decaryana* and *Vanilla madagascariensis* grow together with baobabs. *Microcoelia guyoniana* is an epiphytic orchid that grows deep within African jungles. It is completely stemless and leafless, but its aerial roots* are adapted for chlorophyll conversion.

The natural affinities between plants is also an interesting phenomena. Witness the beautiful Madagascar orchid *Cymbidiella rhodochila,* which grows among *Platycerium madagascariense* ferns. These ferns flourish on *Pandanus utilis,* the vaquois tree, whose leaves are used for weaving baskets. YD

Above: *Orchis mascula* at 7,350 feet (2,240 m), Alpes-Maritimes, France

▮ Humboldt-Bonpland Expeditions

Alexander von Humbolt was born in Prussia in 1769. He studied engineering and devoted his life and his fortune to science. His partner in scientific exploration and discovery was the Frenchman Aimé Jacques Goujaud Bonpland who was born in 1773. After several failed attempts, the two men secured the support of the king of Spain, Charles IV, and in 1799 they set off for Venezuela.

Their mission: to gather botanical samples, in particular orchids. They stopped in Cuba in 1800, and the next year headed for Columbia, then Peru, and on to Inca territory in Mexico.

In 1804, they sailed back to Cuba to recover the thirty-six cases of samples they had deposited there during the course of their travels. The Humboldt-Bonpland expeditions have been called the second discovery of the Americas,*

because they brought back 5,800 plant species to Europe, including 3,600 never previously catalogued.

Their great work, *Plantae aequinoxiales* (1813), contained 120 plates illustrated by the famous botanical artists Pierre Jean François Turpin and Pierre-Antoine Poiteau.

Upon their return, Bonpland became the director of the Empress Josephine's famous Malmaison greenhouses and gardens. YD

Friedrich Georg Weitsch, *Humboldt and Bonpland at the Foot of Mount Chimborazo, Equador,* 1806. Schloss Tegel, Berlin.

■ Hybrids

Orchids frequently hybridize in nature, but the world of botany was nonetheless shaken when John Dominy managed to get an inter-generic hybrid of *Cattleya* and *Laelia*, *Laeliocattleya*, to bloom in 1861. Outraged cries of "unatural coupling" and "against God's order" were heard from some quarters. Dominy had already paved his own way with the inter-species crossing of two *Calanthe* orchids (*C. guttata* and *C. loddigessii*), and the successful flowering of his *Cattleya furcata* and *Cattleya masuca* hybrid in 1856.

The rate of hybrid creation is now several thousand per year, sometimes involving plants that are already hybrids of as many as five different orchid genera. F. W. Burbridge's first list of hybrids (1871) consisted of seventeen names. Starting in 1895, the Sander family instituted a system for registering hybrid names, and "Sander's List of Orchid Hybrids" has been available directly from the Royal Horticultural Society since 1961. The list contains approximately 100,000 hybrids. Many of these are sterile, with meristem* reduplication the only possible method of reproduction.

Nowadays, meristem and in vitro germination techniques are used. Most of the *Cymbidium, Phalaenopsis, Cattleya, Epidendrum, Paphiopedilum, Miltonia, Dendrobium* and *Oncidium* orchids commercially available are hybrids. A great deal of scientific and aesthetic work goes into creating an orchid hybrid, and the results can be breathtaking. Many hybrids produce beautiful flowers, have increased longevity, are disease*

65

HYBRIDS

Left:
Orphys ciliata,
Italy

Right:
Orphys lutea,
France

Orphys ciliata x
Orphys lutea,
France

■ INSECTS

Orchids that are not capable of self-pollination* rely on insects to bear pollen either from plant to plant, or from one of their own flowers or organs to another. Different insects are attracted to different flower scents, or are otherwise compatible with particular orchids. *Gymnadenia, Platanthera,* and *Anacamptis,* for example, must be visited by butterflies or moths with long proboscises. *Anacamptis* orchids have even developed parallel guiding strips that extend from

the base of the labellum.* These strips steer insects towards the pollen masses or pollinia. Some orchids' nectar is easily accessed, usually by members of the wasp family. The nectar is contained in a cup formed at the base of the labellum.

Orchids have complicated and different methods of attracting insects to aid in pollination. For instance, almost every species of *Orphys* attracts only one specific insect, usually a bee from the *Andrena* or *Eucera* genera. But sometimes insects make mistakes. If a busy bee happens upon a different orchid than the one that has specifically evolved to attract it, a new hybrid* can be born, leading to the development of a whole new orchid species. JCG

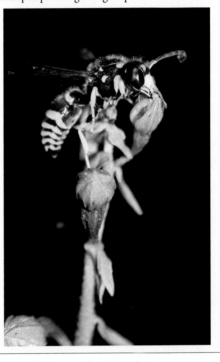

Wasp intoxicated by *Epipactis helleborine,* France

resistant, and adapt more easily to various conditions.

Hybrid names may either be contractions of their parents' designations, or entirely new appellations, such as *Vuylstekeara* and *Wilsonara.* It takes between four and ten years from cross-pollination to the plant's appearance on the market. ML

■ In Vitro Germination

In vitro germination of orchids has been possible since the early twentieth century. Initial work in the area was done by the German mycologist, Hans Burgeff, using fungus, agar gel, and ground salep.* By the 1920s, the American Lewis Knudsen proved that it is possible to germinate orchids without fungus, by substituting synthetic compounds.

Either process can be tried at home, but careful handling, patience and sterile conditions are needed. Hygiene is essential to prevent the spread of microorganisms. Bacteria can both rob the developing orchid of nutrients, and cause fungal or viral diseases.*

Seeds* are sown in a growing medium, usually comprised of agar gel, sugar, water, and other

Facing page:
Platanthera
chlorantha
(green orchid),
France

Indigenous
Serapias
variety, Italy

necessary nutrients. Laboratories often begin the process with agar plus the natural symbiotic* or mycorrhizal fungus. Whether the fungus is used or not, seeds are sealed within a sterilized glass container, usually referred to as a flask, and exposed to light for more than twelve hours a day. They are usually kept at a temperature between 68 and 72° F (20 to 22° C). After a period of between ten days and two months, depending upon the species, germination occurs. Fifteen to eighteen weeks later, the embryo develops into a protocorm, covered with tiny rhizoids.

Six to twelve months and a few changes to fresh sterilized flasks later, the seedlings* are ready to be placed in a fine compost.
Before replanting, they are carefully cleaned, and a fungicide may be applied. At this point they will be about one to three inches (3 to 8 cm) tall, with three to five leaves and a small tangle of roots. For the next few weeks they must be kept in a sterilized propagating case. Extra humidity and warmth is required; 73 to 81° F (23 to 27° C) by day and 64 to 68° F (18 to 20° C) at night. Once pseudobulbs appear or they seem to be hardy enough, the seedlings are ready for replanting. They are then placed in two to three inch (5 to 7 cm) diameter pots, filled with fine compost. A new plant produces increasingly solid looking pseudobulbs until a flowering stem appears. Depending once again upon the species, this can take from two to seven years. The waiting period can be shorter sometimes: *Dendribium microbulbon* has been known to bloom after just nine months. ML

■ Labellum

The labellum (from the Latin for "lip") is one of the orchid's three petals. Its appearance, far more showy and striking than that of the other two, is a major part of the orchid's beauty.
The labellum may form a pouch, as in the lady's slipper* (*Cypripedium calcelous*) or a flat (*Platanthera*) or curling (*Orchis papilionacea*) tongue. The "tongue" may be forked (*Epipactis, Cephalanthera*), double (*Listera ovata, Neottia nidus-avis*), triple (*Dactylorhiza* and many *Orchis*), or even quadruple.

For *Ophrys* orchids, the labellum plays an essential part in pollination.* Many orchids, including the majority of *Orchis* and *Dactylorhiza,* have a prolonged spur which may or may not produce nectar. In *Gymnadenia, Anacamptis, Platanthera,* and *Nigritella,* the spur invariably produces a nectar which attracts insects* for pollination. The labellum is often decorated with a raised pattern of prickles or hairy fibers which act as a sort of landing pad for insects.

An unusual looking labellum is sometimes the basis of an orchid's common or scientific name. *Aceras anthropophorum,* the hanged man orchid, has a labellum that looks like a miniature man. The labellum of *Orchis simia* looks like a beckoning monkey. *Seraphis lingua,* the tongue orchid, has (of course) a tongue-like tip. JCG

■ Lady's Slipper

Of the hundred and forty or so orchid species indigenous to North America, the *Cypripedium* is perhaps the most famous. The genus, whose name means Venus' slipper or foot, is also known by the common* names lady's slipper and moccasin flower. It grows in woodlands, meadows, and marshlands. Lady's slipper species are also found in Asia and Mexico. Only one species (*C. calceolus*) occurs in Europe, although, as in the United States, several varieties of it are found.

Lady's slippers are terrestrial* orchids. Most of them go into a dormant state during the winter months, break through the ground in spring, flower in early summer, and seed when autumn begins. The pouchlike shape of the lady slipper labellum* causes insects* to touch both the male and female organs of the flower.

Although they naturally thrive in all but the very hottest parts of North America, lady's slippers have become scarce in many parts of the United States. *C. reginae,* known as the showy, or the pink and white, lady's slipper, can grow as tall as four ft (1.2 m) and is the Minnesota state flower. However the species is now rare there, and lady's slippers are listed as endangered* species in several states.

They are threatened primarily by the destruction of its habitats, but also by collecting. Those lady's slippers designated "nursery propagated" may have spent only one growing season in a nursery, and been initially lifted from the wild. As with most terrestrial orchids, digging up and transplanting individual lady's slippers found in forests and marshes almost always fails, usually because of root* destruction. One reason for nevertheless attempting to harvest wild lady's slippers may be that flask germination takes about three years.

The most common species of North American lady's slippers include *C. californium,* the white and green ladys slipper; *C. reginae,* which grows in the Northeast and Midwest; varieties of *C. acaule,* which are also those most frequently called moccasin orchids, but also can be known as pink or stemless lady's slippers; and *C. calceolus,* the yellow lady's slipper, which grows consistently throughout North America, as well as in England, France and elsewhere across Europe.

European
*Cypripedium
calceolus,* France

■ LIGHT

 Like all plants, orchids need light. It is essential for photosynthesis, the series of chemical reactions by which vegetation assimilates nutrients.

Light is measured in luces. In regular indoor light, an orchid gets only several hundred of the several thousand luces it normally needs to live. For example, *Paphiopedilum* orchids require between five and ten thousand luces, *Phalaenopsis* between ten and fifteen thousand, *Cymbidium* around fifty thousand, and some *Vanda* orchids need even more light than that. But these figures should not discourage you from trying to grow orchids in your home. Orchids are amazingly adaptable plants, and artificial lighting can easily be used to supplement weak indoor light.

Orchids do well in natural light coming from eastern, southern, or western exposure. Northern exposure is too weak for them. A south-facing window can provide up to twenty thousand luces, and is an ideal spot for orchids, especially in the winter. Eastern and western exposures give plants between three and five thousand

luces. Orchids like to be placed on wide windowsills. From March through late September, the plants should be protected from direct light by a transparent curtain or adjustable blinds. Double-glazed windows cut down the light's strength by twenty-five percent, while moving the plants as little as a 20 inches (50 cm) away from the window pane cuts the available light in half.

Orchids transplanted from outdoors should be carefully protected until they acclimatize* to new surroundings. For them, artificial lighting is a must.

White walls are good for reflecting light on the plants. One lamp is enough to cover two plants. The number of florescent bulbs needed varies in relation to the type and quantity of orchids and where they are grown. Orchids adopt well to artificial lighting, except when a lamp gives off too much heat. In order to maintain a night and day differential, orchids should not be exposed to artificial lighting for more than sixteen hours a day. ML

Artificial lighting in a *Phalaenopsis* greenhouse.
Marcel Lecoufle growers, France.

73

Jacques-Émile Blanche, *Portrait of Marcel Proust,*1892. Oil on canvas. Musée d'Orsay, Paris.

Literature

In Shakespeare's *Hamlet,* some of the flowers in Opheila's famed bouquet may be orchids. Queen Gertrude describes Opheila walking towards the stream where she will drown herself, singing to the "fantastic garlands" she has woven as if for her own grave. Among the flowers mentioned, the reference to "long purples" suggest indigenous English orchids, though it is not clear which species. Two distinct possibilities are *Orchis,* with its highly suggestive tubers, and *Dactylorhiza,* with its otherworldly, finger-like shoots.

In "The Flowering of the Strange Orchid," H. G. Wells tells the story of a timid bachelor who comes upon a marvelous orchid, whose intoxicating perfume makes the bachelor swoon. In the end, he is saved from death in the nick of time, just as the orchid has wound him in its tentacles and is poised to suck the life out of his body. One of the most memorable orchid references in literature is found in Marcel Proust's *Remembrance of Things Past.*

Therewith fantastic garlands did she make
Of crow-flowers, nettles, daisies, and long purples,
That liberal shepherds give a grosser name,
But our cold maids do dead men's fingers call them.

William Shakespeare
Hamlet IV.vii.169–171

The seductive Odette de Crécy's favorite flower is the *Cattleya labiata*, which she wears in her hair and in her bosom, and loves to twist around her fingers. Odette's first amorous encounter with Charles Swann is so centered around this bloom that the couple come to use the phrase "*faire Catleya*" (make *Catleya*) as a euphemism for lovemaking.

And even a hard-boiled detective may be seduced by orchids. Nero Wolfe, the greatest creation of American crime writer Rex Stout, hates adventure of any kind. Instead, he is devoted to three consuming passions: beer, fine food, and orchids. He maintains three separate greenhouses (one for each global temperature range), and every day takes the elevator up to the roof of his Manhattan brownstone to commune with his beloved hothouse "concubines."
YD

▪ Love and Death

Their strange, almost supernatural, appearance has meant that orchids have often been linked with magic and the occult.

In many cultures, orchids are used in love potions or folk remedies. In Madagascar, for instance, the aphrodisiac powers of the stems of a certain vanilla* orchid are so prized that the plant is now nearly extinct. Tribes in southern and tropical Africa use the leafy parts and pseudobulbs of *Ansellia*, a genus of *Ansellia africana*, to make contraceptive bracelets, though they reputedly only work for unmarried women.

In Papua New Guinea, the orchid is believed to have both marital and medicinal benefits: some tribes wrap their baby girls in the leaves of a species of *Habenaria* to instill the health, and capacity for drudgery needed to satisfy a husband. Local legend also recounts the tale of a ghostly lady who wanders naked along the riverbanks, seducing all men in her path; those who don't satisfy her expectations are stricken with venereal diseases that only the *Dendrobium* can cure.

The orchid can also be as deadly as it is beautiful. In some parts of the Mediterranean, orchid tubers are used to make a potion known as "the hand of death." In Mexico, *Bletia reflexa* is called the "flower of death." Historical accounts of human sacrifice in northern Australia report that victims were anointed with the juice of local pseudobulbs before being slain. Mixed with other substances, the tubers of some species of *Habenaria* make a supposedly deadly potion, though the orchid may not be the active ingredient.

With blushes bright as morn fair Orchis charms
And lulls her infant in her fondling arms;
Soft plays Affection round her bosom's throne,
And guards his life, forgetful of her own.
So wings the wounded deer her headlong flight,
Pierced by some ambush'd archer of the night,
Shoots to the woodlands with her bounding fawn,
And drops of blood bedew the conscious lawn;
There, hid in shades, she shuns the cheerful day,
Hangs o'er her young, and weeps her life away.

From *The Loves of the Plants*, Erasmus Darwin

Title page from Rembert Dodoens' *History of Plants, Containing a Complete Description of Herbs*, Antwerp, 1657.

Medicine

In the first century C.E., the Greek herbalist Discorides* associated orchid roots with human fertility and theorized that physical disorders should be treated with plants that most resembled the ailing body part. The orchid tuber's supposed visual similarity to male genitalia led to its association with virility and potency, a correlation which persists to this day.

Orchids have been extensively used for medicinal purposes throughout Asia. In China, Japan, and Tibet, *Bletilla* orchids have been prized as blood purifiers and mood enhancers. During the Chinese Han Dynasty (207 B.C.E.–220 C.E.) an essence made from the dried pseudobulbs of *Dendrobium nobile* was considered effective in balancing the body's energy and the orchid was widely farmed for this purpose. Through the early nineteenth century, an extract of *Dactylorhiza maculata* was prescribed in European counties to cure tuberculosis. In North America, several species of *Cypripedium* were used to treat inflammations and skin ailments. North American species of *Epipactis*

Cymbidium dayanum, South East Asia

was widely prescribed for nervous disorders, and listed in the official publication *United States Pharmacopoeia.*

In some places, the medicinal properties of such orchid derivatives as vanilla,* salep,* and faham are still sworn by today. Dried faham leaves are, for example, drunk in tea form as a digestive, and smoked to prevent asthma attacks. GC

Meristem

A meristem is a group of unspecialized cells capable of division and found at the tip of a plant stem or root. In meristem cultivation a plant—carefully chosen for its quality—divides into a great many identical offspring. These stem cells are and can become specialized to form new plant tissue. This method, first developed in orchids by the French botanist Georges Morel, in 1960, is used to grow housands of identical orchids are grown in specialized greenhouses.*

A meristem is first placed in an enriched growing compound. Once the embryo stage is reached, it is transferred to a new environment similar to the kind used for in vitro germination. Meristem production has made the price of orchids much more reasonable. Orchids grown from seedlings take up to six years to flower, but a meristem orchid blooms at the end of three years, or sooner. Some varieties, such as *Phalaenopsis,* will flower after only eighteen months.

Certain types of orchids, such as *Paphiopedilum,* are not well suited to meristem reproduction, but orchids to be sold cut are often grown this way, particularly *Cybidium, Dendrobium,* and *Phalaenopsis.* ML

■ Moisture

Most orchids thrive in humid conditions. The greater the distance from the equator, where levels are stable, the more the humidity fluctuates with the seasons. Different orchids thus require different levels of moisture; for instance, pseudobulbous and hard leafed orchids require more than those without pseudobulbs or soft leaves.

Overall, there are simple ways to satisfy orchids' basic needs. One is by placing their pots in high rimmed draining basins or saucers filled with pebbles or clay pellets. Let a half inch (1 cm) or so of water stand at the bottom at each watering. Your orchids will then be able to enjoy the

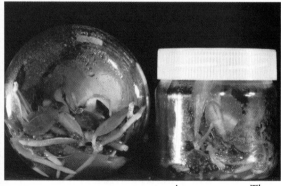

Meristem cultivation of *Phalaenopsis*

excess water as it evaporates. Pots must be placed on top of the pellets, never in the water itself. Standing water in pots leads to directly to the decay of young plants. *Phalaenopsis* and *Paphiopedilium* are particularly vulnerable to this.

Orchids thrive in 60 percent humidity, and suffer if the humidity level drops below 40 percent. Humid conditions diminish moisture loss through evaporation. It is an absolute no-no to increase watering* of dried out orchids. This will only lead to root* rot.

The saucer-pellet-pot technique works well on a windowsill, where orchids will appreciate the light.* Daily room temperature* watering (in season and with water that is not too hard or too soft) is very good for orchids. When spraying, use the finest mist possible, and do not aim the spray directly at the flowers or the core of the plant. Avoid misting in strong sunlight, since it can cause brown spots to appear on the leaves. ML

■ Neumann, Joseph

Charles Darwin's* studies on reproduction in plants explained the importance of insects* to *Vanilla fragrans* pollination, yet no European botanical* garden could manage to bring vanilla orchids to bear fruit after flowering.* In the end, it was advances in artificial pollination* that revolutionized the vanilla market.

In artificial pollination, up to fifteen hundred flowers can be pollinated in a single morning. The labellum* is simply lowered and torn to uncover the column. The anther cap is then lifted with a needle, toothpick, or palm leaf fiber and placed under the stamen. At this point, pressing a finger puts the pollen grains in contact with the stigmatic surface, the sticky area made to receive it.

According to some accounts, the first true and practical method of artificial pollination* was performed in 1841 by Edmund Albius,a former slave on the French colonial island of Réunion. Others cite the Frenchman Joseph Neumann as the first to succeed, in 1830, just a few years before the other contenders. GC

Orchid Hunters

Orchids, particularly endemic terrestrial* varieties, were of little interest to Europeans before the discovery of tropical epiphytes.* The discovery of stunning tropical varieties was met with tremendous enthusiasm.

The first orchids to reach Europe in the sixteenth century were more or less dried samples. Eagerness to obtain living plants was great—expeditions were launched and large sums of money were invested, often with expectations of great financial gain.

Orchids were sold at exorbitant prices, but the cost in ecological terms was far more devastating. Desperate to meet demand, orchid hunters pillaged forests and destroyed rare plant populations. Ironically, transportation and cultivation know-how remained limited up until the nineteenth century, and the majority of orchids collected died in transport.

In the 1830s, Nathaniel Ward's invention of small glass and wood greenhouses made for fewer plant casualties in transportation. The Ward boxes quickly became common on ships carrying orchids as cargo. At the same time, the work of Noël Bernard* and Joseph Neumann* ushered in improvements in hybrid* cultivation which soon made orchid hunting obsolete.

Contemporary orchid hunters must be extremely careful not to harm plants or damage habitats.* They are subject to stringent local and international laws, such as those stipulated by the CITES agreement.* While environmental destruction is a serious problem, conservation* efforts are in effect throughout the world and many orchids

are listed as endangered* or protected species.

Botanists who are orchid specialists continue to work on the same issues as their predecessors. They study the extents and characteristics of endemic biosystems, and how specific species reproduce. And they use mini-traveling greenhouses (usually flasks) to provide samples to botanical gardens throughout the world. YD

Vanilla flower, Polynesia

■ Outdoor Growing

A quarter of all orchids are terrestrial,* meaning they grow with their roots* in the ground. Terrestrial orchids are generally indigenous to temperate or cold regions, including Europe, northern Asia, North America, and Australia. They can be grown on terraces or in gardens. Terrestrial species of *Cypripedium, Orchis, Dactylorhiza,* and *Ophrys* can be grown outdoors. Protection from wind and too much sun is required, but the true difficulty lies in recreating their particular native soil. No ready made compost* is available to do the job, and different species require different combinations of materials.

Dactylorhiza foliosa growing in the ground

Soil containing clay and enriched with oak or beech leaf humus, with coarse sand, pine bark, and compost added in the right quantity, can work for *Ophrys, Orchis,* and *Dactylorhiza.* Most species of *Cypripedium calceolus* (lady's slipper) prefer chalky soil. Many other *Cypripedium* and *Spiranthes* species prefer more acidic soil which can be obtained by substituting sphagnum moss for the sand and bark.

Some Asian species (*Pleione* and *Bletilla*) can adapt to mild European and North American climates, if they are protected in winter. They prefer partial shade, and soil mixed with pine bark and peat. ML

A duped insect
(Chalicodoma sp.)
pollinating an
Ophrys bertoloni

■ POLLINATION
A Bag of Tricks

Pollination is the transfer of a flower's pollen (male sex cells) to the stigma (the female sexual organ) of another flower for fertilization. This is done with the help of insects,* hummingbirds, or even bats.

Orchids have a broad array of methods to attract pollinators. The pollen grains form a clump or pollinium which sticks to the back or head of the pollinator. When it makes its way to the female stigma of another flower, the pollinium is released, resulting in what is called crossed pollination.

Ophrys, a genus of orchids native to Europe and the Middle East, uses its shiny, reflective labellum* to entice to male wasps, bees, and hornets, who mistake it for the female of their species. The orchid also produces a scent which the excitable male takes to be the odor of a female counterpart. The duped insect lands on the orchid's labellum and is coated in pollen as it attempts to copulate. When it gives up and flies away, the insect immediately spots another illusory mate, and releases the pollen there.

There are orchids (such as *Gymnadenia, Anacamptis, Platanthera, Nigritella,* and certain *Orchis*) that attract insects with a heavily perfumed nectar. Orchids without nectar (such as *Listera, Coeloglossum, Aceras,* and many *Epipactis*) have to rely on have other wiles. Some produce a sweet amino acid coating which covers the stigmatic surface destined to receive the pollen. There are even rare cases where the nectar and sweet coating combine in a process of fermentation, literally intoxicating the insects pollinators. Insects can become addicted to this alcohol, and repeatedly visit the orchids that provide it.

Orchids may help insects in their work by making a sort of landing pad out of their labellums, or may have bag-shaped labellums which leave trapped insects only one way out: brushing past the pollinia.

Unwilling to trust in their own powers of seduction and leave the rest to nature, there are also stubborn orchids that self-pollinate. For some orchid genera, the method of pollination is not yet known, and further study continues to uncover greater mysteries. JCG and ML

 In addition to seed and in vitro cultivation, there are a few ways to propagate orchids from existing plants. Large orchids, such as *Cymbidium, Cattleya,* and *Vanda,* can be divided into two or more parts when their seasonal regrowth periods begin. A plant must reach a certain level of maturity before it can be successfully divided, and too many divisions will result in weakened duplicates. A sympodial orchid, which puts out creeping shoots from a rhizome, should not be divided before it has six to eight pseudobulbs, and the rhizome should be cut between two pseudobulbs.

Monopodial orchids, which form buds on a stem, should be cut below a cluster of at least three aerial roots. If the plant is tall but has no aerial roots, they can be forced by making incisions in the stem and coating them with cutting compound. Division should be done only once the aerial roots have developed.

Orchids with cane-like stalks, such as *Dendrobium nobile,* can be grown from cuttings. Simply cut old stems without flowers or leaves into four to six inch (10 to 15 cm) pieces, and lay them in damp peat moss in a humid greenhouse environment.

Cymbidium, Cattleya, Odontoglossum, and some other orchids have dormant pseudobulbs (backbulbs) which store nutrients for the active pseudobulbs. These can be brought to life using several different methods, but it can take months for a new shoot to form. Make sure there is at least one dormant bud or "eye" on the pseudo-bulbous base.

Any cutting should be done with ster-ilized tools to minimize the risk of viral infection, and fungicide powder should be dusted on all incisions. Once repotted, the new plants should be attached to stakes* to help them grow upright. ML

Dendrobium nobile

83

Miltonia hybrid

■ Repotting

Although most orchids are epi-phytic,* and could therefore thrive on any surface to which their roots* can attach, indoors, orchids are conventionally grown in pots. Many orchid lovers prefer synthetic to clay pots, because they are light and more easy to keep clean and sterilize. Unlike clay pots, plastic containers don't accumulate mineral buildups which can be harmful to orchid roots.* In addition, roots do not stick to a plastic pot's inner surface, and this keeps them from breaking in repotting. Because they are

Removal from old pot without damaging roots

Clipping dead roots

Repotting without covering pseudobulbs and rhizomes

light-weight, larger synthetic pots often need to be weighted so as not to topple when large, heavy orchids are grown in them. Large epiphytic and pendulous species are often best off in metal, wooden, or plastic baskets, or mounted on bark, cork, or logs.

Orchids like cramped containers, and should only be repotted when necessary. The main reasons for repotting are deteriorated compost,* damaged roots, or roots that overflow the pot to the point of drying out. To check on the roots, tap the pot on a ledge to remove the compost and plant in one swift movement. Brown and dried out or rotted roots call for a change. To begin repotting, first lift the plant completely out of the pot without damaging the roots. Then clip away dead parts and dust the cuts with fungicide powder. Sterilize the new pot, which should be the same size or just slightly larger than the old one. Cover the bottom with an inch or two (2 to 5 cm) of pellets or pebbles. Add a layer of moist compost, and set the plant on it. The pseudobulbs and rhizomes should be just barely covered. Cover all roots with compost. Carefully insert stakes* to train the stalk and keep it from falling down and breaking. Lightly water* or spray the plant for the first two weeks, until new roots appear.

Repotting is best done in the spring (for *Paphiopedilum)* or the end of the dormant period (for *Cybidium* and *Cattleya)* when new roots sprout. Monopodial orchids (such as *Phalaenopsis* and *Vanda)*, grow continuously. They can be repotted in any season except winter. Never reuse compost in repotting. ML

■ Roots

The underground portions of terrestrial* orchids consist of roots and an underground rhizome or tuber which allows for the growth of new plants without pollination.* Although they are generally called bulbs, they are not actually so. In some terrestrial orchids, the nutrient reserve organ is a pseudobulb formed by a bulge in the stem.

Orchid roots are cylindrical, whitish or brownish filaments which rarely branch. They grow below the tuber, hold the plant in place and are a conduit for nutrients. In terrestrial temperate

Tuber of an *Orchis morio* (green winged orchid)

Rhizomes of a *Neottia nidus-avis* (bird's nest orchid)

zone orchids with short rhizomes or no tubers, the rhizome's roots can form into closely configured, interlaced balls that resemble birds' nests (*Neottia)* or golf clubs (*Limodorum).*

The tuber is a fleshy mass which produces a plant capable of flowering and bearing fruit. A second tuber develops in tandem with the first, to replace it

Facing page:
Phaius fruit,
splitting open

after blooming. This second tuber stores the nutrients needed for growth in the following year. Tuber shape differs from genus to genus. They are oval or globular in *Ophrys* and *Orchis,* and palm or hand shaped in *Dactylorhiza, Gymnadenia, Nigritella,* and *Coeloglossum.* Plants without tubers may have a rhizome, the subterranean stem with attached roots that grows parallel to the ground. Tubers get their nourishment from the top layers of humus. Forest species such as *Cypripedium, Epipactis,* and *Cephalanthera* have tubers. Each year, the tuber gets longer, and its older portions die off. Rhizomes produces buds which rise above ground to form flowering shoots.

Epiphytic* orchids have aerial roots that enable them to take nourishment and to support themselves perched on other plants, often trees. JCG

■ Salep

Salep is a starchy foodstuff* made in the Near East from the tubers of several species of *Orchis.* Salep was at one time popular in India, parts of China, and Europe. Today it is still produced in Turkey and Greece. It is credited with a variety of health benefits, and is believed to increase virility. The Turkish common names for the tubers attest to this: *Orchis hircina* and *Orchis mascula* are known as "dog testicle" and "fox testicle" respectively.

Powdered salep can be mixed with honey or figs to make a highly valued drink, though its popularity is thankfully restricted. It takes up to two hundred thousand orchids to fill a 110 pound (50 kg) bag of salep tubers, and widespread

enthusiasm for salep surely mean extinction for the orchids in question. YD

■ Seeds

It is hard to find orchid seeds at the local nursery, and in any event, the germination process requires so much time and care that many orchid lovers opt for other propagation methods. Still, orchid societies* associations, and clubs have created seed banks for their members.

After blooming and pollination,* the peduncle transforms into a seed bearing capsule. This process can happen as quickly as twenty-seven days (*Ludisia discolor*), or as take as long as twenty-six months (*Coelogyne cristata*). Upon maturity the capsule usually turns yellow and cracks open. In nature, millions of these minute seeds (weighing 3 to 6 m) are dispersed by the wind. To prevent seed loss and contamination that would spoil in vitro germination, capsules of cultivated orchids are covered before being harvested. Orchid seeds cannot survive for more than a few months.

Because orchids are monocotyledons, their seeds lack self-sustaining nutrient reserves. Instead, they consist of an embryo with thirty-odd cells and a minute quantity of nutritive matter, all bundled in a sheer, translucent skin. In the wild, a fungus penetrates the embryonic seed, creating a symbiotic relationship.* As the fungus consumes minerals from the soil, the embryo begins to digest the fungus and develop. In most in vitro germination, the minerals and sugars necessary for development, rather than the fungus itself, are added to an agar gel. ML

110 pounds
(50 kg) of orchid
tubers for salep
preparation,
Turkey

Orchid seeds* are the smallest of all monocotyledon seeds. Since the tiny seed provides the embryo with only a minuscule amount of nutrients, a fungus is need to help nourish the fledgling organism. The seeds inflate with water and burst, allowing the *Rhizoctonia* fungus to penetrate embryo cells. Supplied with nutrients from the fungus, the cells begin to multiply. In most cases, the mass of cells gradually weans itself of this symbiotic relationship* when photosynthesis begins. As shoot and roots* form, the young orchid slowly begins to resemble a plant. The fungus is relegated to the roots, where remains during the orchid's adult phase.

Orchid seeds can be sown in vitro. The operation must be carried out in laboratory-like conditions. Along with all the items to be used, the seeds themselves have to be sterilized. The sowing medium is agar, and seeds from a particular source should be divided among several flasks or jars for germination so that any contamination will not affect all the others.

In professional laboratories, the rate of success is 95 percent. Experienced amateurs succeed 50 to 80 percent of the time. Beginners manage to pull it off only 10 percent of the time, but—as always—practice can make perfect. ML

Cattleya labiata, autumnalis variety, Brazil
Following pages: *Cattleya elongata,* Brazil

■ SEXUAL REPRODUCTION

A wide range of flora, including fungi, seaweed, ferns, moss, and lichen, have discreet sexual parts and means of reproduction known as cryptogams. More evolved flowering plant forms, including orchids, reproduce with greater fanfare. The first to write in depth on the topic was the French botanist Sébastien Vaillant (1669-1722), whose writings on pollination* at times reach a pitch of

frenzied excitement. Plant sexuality was also studied in the nineteenth century by Charles Darwin,* Joseph Neumann* and other distinguished scientists.

It was Darwin who definitively deduced and detailed the intricacies of orchid pollination in his book *On the Various Contrivances by Which British and Foreign Orchids Are Fertilized by Insects,* a work of which he was particularly proud. One story has it that Darwin began formulating his theories during a walk in the Devonshire countryside. First observing the strange dance of insects* around orchids, he went on to prove that the plants specifically attracted the insects for use in pollination. YD

Above: *Ophrys tenthredinifera,* Spain
Below: *Cattleya araguaiensis,* South America

■ Societies

The first orchid society was founded in England in 1897. Ever since, associations of this kind have steadily multiplied. These groups promote orchid awareness of all kinds: from information about species and growing techniques, to lobbying for extended protection for endangered* orchids. Orchid societies provide a wide range of services which are useful for beginning house plant owners and specialized botanists alike. The major orchid society in the United States is the American Orchid Society. It acts as a coordinator for the hundreds of orchid societies throughout the country, and publishes the *American Orchid Society Bulletin,* a treasure trove of the latest

■ Spontaneous Propagation

Under certain conditions, orchids perpetuate their species' continued existence without having to go through the long seed germination process. They produce spontaneous growths called *keikis,* after the Hawaiian word for baby. A *keiki* can sprout anywhere on an orchid plant,

orchid information. The Canadian Orchid Congress, the British Orchid Council, and the South African Orchid Council similarly coordinate the activities of the many orchid societies in their respective countries. On the international level, this role is fulfilled by the World Orchid Conference Trust, the International Orchid Commission, and other inclusive organizations.

In light of the still-increasing threat that industrialization, pollution, and other factors pose to orchids, orchid societies play a vital role in representing and advancing the flower's plight. ML

from root* to pseudobulb to flowering stalk. They are the fortuitous effects of imperfect growing conditions, such as excessive heat, over-watering, too much rain, or too little light.*

Once its roots reach about two inches (5 cm), a *keiki* can be gently removed, dusted with fungicide powder, and repotted* in fine-grade compost.* A *keiki* will be a natural clone of the original plant, exactly identical to it. They mature to the point of blooming sooner than a plant grown from seed, and most commonly occur in *Phalaenopsis, Vanda,* and *Dendrobium* orchids.

Keiki on a
Phalaenopsis
Luettemannia

Keiki on a *Dendrobium topaziacum*

Spontaneous propagation also takes place when a home or commercially grown orchid seed pod bursts open before it is harvested. The seeds land in surrounding pots and sometimes germinate, forming new plants that take several years to reach maturity. If the plants are the result of hybridization,* flowers can be a different color from those of the parent plant. Orchids can spontaneously propagate outdoors as well, if they are indigenous or acclimatized* to the area. Ordinary plowing can also result in creating large patches of some particular sort of

Attaching a *Vuylstekeara cambria*

orchid, since it can spread seeds and shoots. ML

■ Stakes

In the wild, orchid flowers droop unless they are supported by rigid bulbs, as is the case with *Cattleya* and *Laelia.* If you consider that the inflorescence, or flowering pattern, of *Oncidium* occurs on stalks that can reach six feet (2 m) in length, the practicality of staking becomes apparent. Some drooping or pendulous orchids, though, will not tolerate training.

Stakes are also useful for supporting plants during transport. Since the majority of dead or damaged roots* are removed before repotting,* staking can be helpful in holding plants in place as they settle and take hold in new compost.* The stakes should be thin, and made of wood or plastic. After carefully inserting the stake in the compost so as not to harm the roots, attach the stalk to the stake with twist-ties or raffia. Once a plant has settled into its new pot and developed new roots, the stake may then be removed. ML

Left:
"burgundian"
Cymbidium

■ A SYMBIOTIC RELATIONSHIP

 Symbiosis is a relationship where two organisms join together for mutual benefit. In what is known as a mycorrhizal association, orchids house strand-like mycorrhiza fungi in their root cells, and in return get nutrients synthesized by the fungi. Tiny orchid seeds* lack albumen, and need the help of a fungus to germinate. The fungus remains indispensable to the orchid for the remainder of its existence. Fungi in the *Rhizoctonia* genre affect only the peripheral root* areas of the plant, and are destroyed if they go deeper. They are not present in the tuber or above ground parts of the plant. In tuber orchids, such as *Orchis* and *Ophrys,* when an old tuber dies the fungus transfers to the roots of the new tuber, allowing the development of the shoot that will become a tuber in the following year.

Sometimes symbiosis is permanent, and the fungus provides the plant with vital hydrocarbons. Although mature orchids are capable of getting all the nutrients they need through photosynthesis, plants can still become dependant on fungi for these needs. Symbiosis can even lead to a loss of chlorophyll, when a plant no longer needs green leaves for synthesis. This is the case with saprophytic orchids which get their nutrients from humus in the forest. They include the ghost orchid, *Epipogium aphyllum*; the bird's nest orchid, *Neottia nidus-avius*; the coral orchid *Corallorhiza*; and the Australian *Rhizanthella* which lives almost completely underground, with its flowers barely poking through the surface. JCG

Neottia nidus-avis (bird's nest orchid)
Savoy, France.

Edgar Maxence, *Woman with an Orchid,* 1900. Musée d'Orsay, Paris.

◼ Symbolism: Beauty, Art, and Potency

In China, orchids have always been loved for their beauty, as well as for their symbolic and medicinal uses. The anthropologist Jack Goody has discussed how from the Sung dynasty (960–1279 C.E.) to the present, spiritual connections between beings are viewed as a "sacred orchid link." Confucius himself likened meeting a virtuous person to stepping into a room full of the subtle yet powerful scent of orchids.

Orchids play an important part throughout Chinese painting. In Sheng Su-hsaio's paintings of the Mongolian invasions (1250–1300 C.E.), for instance, the uprooting of orchids is depicted as the "rape" of Chinese soil. The late seventeenth-century Chinese painting manual *Chieh Tzu Yuan Hua Chuan* devotes many pages to the history and techniques of orchid painting. And while the tradition of depicting orchids in art is much less developed in the West, Georgia O'Keeffe's luscious paintings of orchid flowers are a notable example.

Around the world, orchids have long been symbols of fertility and potency. In ancient Greece, for instance, orchid tubers were associated with male genitalia, as the legend of Orchis reflects. A young man who raped a priestess, Orchis was torn to shreds by wild beasts. Afterwards, his sexual organs became tuberous roots and orchid flowers sprouted from his remains. Less violent is the Japanese account of *Cymbidium ensiflium* or "thirteen great treasures." Upon smelling this orchid, an empress was cured of infertility, and gave birth to a succession of thirteen children. YD

A *Brassia verrucosa* from Mexico or Venezuela

Spiranthes spiralis

■ Temperate Zone Orchids

Orchids, like all flowering plants, are comprised of reproductive and vegetative portions. The reproductive parts are the flower and fruit, the vegetative parts include the stalks, leaves, and roots,* whether tubers or rhizomes.

Many orchids from the temperate regions of Europe and North America are herbaceous, with considerable differences in morphology and size. They do not bifurcate, and consist of cylindrical flowers that are rarely jagged or prickly. In some species, stems are swollen (*Nigritella, Liparis*), while they are often hollow in others (varieties of *Dactylorhiza*). Stems may be smooth or fuzzy.

Leaves may be clustered together in rosettes at the foot of the stem (*Ophrys*) or distributed along its length. There is also great variety in the quantity and shape of leaves. The adder's mouth orchid, *Malaxis monophyllos*, has one predominant leaf. *Genmaria diphylla* and *Platanthera bifolia* sport two.

There are orchids with ovoid leaves (*Listera ovata*), heart shaped leaves (*Listera cordata*), very small leaves (*Epipactis microphylla*), and lanceolate leaves (*Cephalanthera longifolia*). In almost all, the leaves have parallel veins, although *Goodyera repens* leaves are reticulated. And (except for saprophytic orchids) they are usually green, or may have brown spots, as in *Dactylorhiza maulata*.

Their flowers are usually cylindrical, but they may be spherical (*Traunsteinera globosa*), pyramid shaped (*Anacamptis puramidalis*), or spiraled (*Spiranthes spiralis*). Blooms* appear at the intersection of a small leaf called a bract, and the stem tip. In some cases there is only one flower, in others two (*Cypripedium calceolus*), and sometimes they develop into spikes. Some are saprophytic, meaning that they do not produce chlorophyll through photosynthesis; instead they consume needed nutrients underground, from decaying or dead matter. The coral orchid, *Corallorhiza*, and the bird's nest orchid, *Neottia nidus-avius*, are prime examples of this. JCG

Cephalanthera damasonium (formerly *C. pallens*). Plate from Jean-Baptiste Barla's *Orchid Iconography*, Nice, 1868.

Cephalanthera pallens C. L. Rich.

■ TEMPERATURE

In the nineteenth century, the first orchids brought to Europe were placed in greenhouses* which supposedly simulated a hot equatorial climate. At the time it was not understood that high altitudes in equatorial and tropical zones have cooler temperatures. In fact, whether growing in a natural habitat, an apartment, or a greenhouse setting, orchids require a sizeable shift in day and nighttime temperatures. Although most orchids can adapt to temperatures between 64 and 68° F (18 to 20° C), they usually need a lower nighttime temperature in order to do well.

Hot greenhouse orchids such as *Phalaenopsis* and *Cattleya* need a nightly minimum of 58° F (14.5° C), and temperate greenhouse varieties, including most hybrids,* require 55° F (13° C) at night. Cold greenhouse orchids such as *Cymbidium* need the temperature to drop to 50° F (10° C). During the dormant phase, tropical orchids should be keep slightly cooler than these nightly guidelines, since watering* and moisture* are also lower. A thermometer hung beside the plants is useful for monitoring temperature. A sudden accidental drop in nighttime temperature may not have negative consequences. But temperature changes do directly affect growth, and can cause the spontaneous propagation* of *keikis,* or impair blooming.

In mixed temperature greenhouses, which are warm on the lower level and hot higher up, hot greenhouse orchids should be kept on the higher levels, and frequently misted in summer to control overheating and to increase humidity. The orchids should be shaded from direct sunlight and well-ventilated, but never exposed to drafts. ML

Orchid farm, Thailand

*Serapias
vomeracea,*
France

■ Terrestrial

Terrestrials orchids, which grow with their roots underground like most other plants, are a minority in the orchid family. Unlike epiphytic* orchids, they go through dormant cycles and must be allowed to rest during what corresponds to cold or dry seasons. Terrestrials store reserve nutrients in their underground tubers or fleshy roots.* Many of these more humble, less exotic (but often surprising looking) orchids grow in the wild in Europe and temperate parts of North America. They are homespun but not homely, and their allure has caused near-extinction for some species. Legislation now exists against picking these orchids. Today, several species of *Cypripedium* orchids (or lady's slippers), once abundant in woodland and mountain areas, are endangered and protected.

Paphiopedilum is a genus that resembles *Cypripedium,* but is native to the tropics of India and Southeast Asia. It is usually terrestrial. *Lycaste* and *Anguloa,* both indigenous to Central and South America, are also generally terrestrial orchids. There are also many semi-terrestrial or lithophytic orchids, which grow on rocks or stone. YD

■ Traveling Botanists

The European fascination with orchids grew alongside imperialist expansionism in the late-eighteenth and nineteenth centuries. Often backed by wealthy aristocrat patrons, botanists traveled around the globe, collecting observations and species.

The first and perhaps the greatest of the botanist adventurers was Joseph Banks (1743–1820).

John Hamilton Mortimer, *James Cook, Joseph Banks and Lord Sandwich*, c. 1771. Oil on canvas. National Library of Australia, Canberra.

Upon the death of his father, Banks inherited a huge fortune. He soon dropped his studies at Oxford, engaged the astronomer and botanists Israel Lyons as his private tutor, and set out to explore.

Subsequently chosen to direct a Royal Society expedition to the South Seas under the command of James Cook, Banks lavishly contributed his own money to outfit the ship with the finest personnel and equipment available, including four artists to make illustrations, and a staff of servants. The three-year voyage of the H.M.S. *Endeavour* served as a prototype for botanical expeditions to come. Cook and Banks sailed as far as New Zealand and returned to England with about 3,000 plants formerly unknown to Europe, many orchids among them.

In 1771, King George III appointed Banks royal scientific advisor and honorary director of the new Royal Botanic Gardens at Kew. Banks devoted the remainder of his life to his goal of making Kew the world's finest botanical garden.*

The Swede Olof Peter Swartz (1760–1818) was the first true

Hooker (1817-1908) was born into botany. Hooker spend much of his long life roaming the world in search of new plants. Like Banks before him, Hooker set out in grand style, in his case on an extended expedition to India and the Himalayas, whose flora was little known to Europeans at the time. One of Hooker's most important contributions to botany was his work on the role of altitude in plant distribution. YD

▪ Vanilla History

The Aztecs were not the first to enjoy vanilla in Mexico; they acquired a taste for it when they conquered some of their Totonacan neighbors. The Aztec termed it *tlixochitl,* a compound of *tlili,* black, and *xochitl,* fruit. For the Aztec ruler Montezuma, vanilla was an aphrodisiac, and enhanced the flavor of his favorite chocolate drink. The explorer Hernán Cortés brought the black fruit to Europe. It was later christened vanilla by Spanish colonizers in Mexico, who derived the name from the Latin *vagina,* meaning pod or sheath.

orchid specialist. After completing his studies at the age of twenty-three, Swartz traveled through the Americas,* where he collected numerous species. Elected president of the Stockholm Academy, Swartz counted among his greatest achievements a botanical study, *Flora Indiae Occidentalis* (1797-1806), which described thirteen genera and twenty-seven species of West Indian Orchids.

The son of Sir William Jackson Hooker, the first official director of the Royal Botanic Gardens of Kew, Joseph Dalton

Fifty years after its arrival in Europe,* vanilla was only consumed by the very rich in Spain, where it was drunk in combination with cocoa. At the turn of the seventeenth century Hugh Morgan, the royal apothecary to Queen Elizabeth I, realized that vanilla could have wider applications, especially as a flavoring. In Europe and North America, vanilla was prescribed over the centuries for a variety of ailments, from convulsions to menstrual pain to male impotence. One of its first and lasting uses in Europe was in perfume.

Following pages:
Vanilla pods being sorted, Madagascar

After Joseph Neumann's* discovery of artificial pollination,* European commerce in vanilla increased, and cultivation was begun on a large scale in several tropical colonies. In 1897, Mexico was still producing half of the world's vanilla. French colonies overtook the market by 1912, producing about three-fifths of all vanilla. Mexican vanilla maintained its edge in quality and fetched higher prices until about 1940, when the French colonies began to consistently rival it. Today the best vanilla in the world comes from Madagascar, and the Comoros and Seychelles islands, and is known as Bourbon vanilla, after the former name of Madagascar. GC

■ The Vanilla Trade

On a 1676 expedition in Mexico, the English explorer William Dampier first observed the browning of *Vanilla planifola* (also known as *Vanilla fragrans* and Mexican vanilla) vanilla beans.* Pods were either dried in the sun and then coated with oil, or they were immersed in hot water before being sun-dried. Despite repeated efforts to raise vanilla outside the Americas, it was not until after Neumann's* discovery of artificial pollination techniques in 1830 that successful cultivation of vanilla really began.

Cultivation in Tahiti started in 1848, followed by New Caledonia in

VANILLE BOURBON
EXTRA EN POUDRE PURE
Boîte N°   Brut K°   Tare K°   Net K°
ÉTABLISSEMENTS
ANTOINE CHIRIS
PARIS   MARSEILLE
Ac
COMORES - MADAGASCAR - ILE DE BOURBON
IMPORTATION DIRECTE

1861, the Seychelles islands in 1866, and the Comoros in 1873. The French colonies of Réunion (then known as Bourbon Island) and Madagascar (then known as Nossi-Bé) exported 110 pounds of vanilla (50 kg) in 1848, and 45 pounds (20 kg) in 1878, all of it grown from "Mexican vanilla."

By 1940, French colonies and protectorates had overtaken Mexico in vanilla production. Madagascar, along with the Comoros and Seychelles islands, is now the largest producer, and their vanilla is considered the best in the world. Together with Indonesia, the next largest producer, these islands are responsible for 90 percent of world production. *Vanilla fragrans* vanilla from Mexico is considered creamy and spicy. *Vanilla tahitensis,* or Tahitian vanilla, is one of the two other sorts of vanilla orchids that are commercially grown for flavoring. It has a flowery, slightly licorice taste and is sometimes used to aromatize teas and tobacco.

Vanilla from Madagascar is still called Bourbon vanilla. The tried and true technique for making Bourbon vanilla involves scalding beans for three minutes directly after picking, then, while they are still hot, placing them in a plastic and wool coated chamber for heated drying. Next, they are placed on racks to air dry for up to six weeks, receiving alternate periods of sun and shade, before being washed and sealed in cases to give off their oil. The entire process usually takes eight weeks.

Vanilla flavor has also been synthetically produced since 1874. But the natural product remains superior, of course. GC

Orchids like good ventilation. Well circulated fresh air prevents bacterial and fungal diseases* which develop under stuffy conditions. The appearance of unsightly black spots on *Phalaenopsis* flowers is a sign of *Botrytis cinerea,* a fungus that attacks when ventilation is poor.

Ventilation must be carefully set up in order to avoid harmful drafts. To test whether a fan is needed, four inch (10 cm) wool threads can be attached to plants on different levels. If the thread moves, this means that enough air is circulating around the orchid. If you have a growing collection of orchids, a small fan can be placed at a distance to make the threads gently move. Some species, such as *Masdevallia,* need far more air than others.

In heat, ventilation helps lower the temperature,* allowing for less frequent misting. Greenhouses,* even small ones, should be equipped with side and ceiling fans. Slatted openings with fresh air blowers behind them are ideal. Because they can be drying, ventilation systems should never be on the same level as the plants. In summer the greenhouse door can be opened, but this may let in parasites and create drafts. Another option is to put the plants outdoors, making sure to shade them from direct sunlight and wind as needed.

Good ventilation is a must year round, including in winter. Even if this makes the air a bit chilly, orchids prefer movement to warmth. Temperature can be regulated with proper precautions. ML

Phalaenopsis greenhouse, Marcel Lecoufle growers, France.

"Edna Normandy," a *Vuylstekeara* hybrid

■ Watering

Watering cultivated orchids can be complicated. Many species come from tropical climates where intense rainy seasons alternate with dry ones: germination and growing periods require extremely wet conditions, while less water is needed as pseudobulbs are developing and just before blooming. In any case, both diseased* and rooting* plants should be given very little water.

Watering methods differ for orchids grown in pots, baskets, or on other surfaces. Orchids not in pots must be sprayed daily, and submerged once or twice a week; more frequently in summer. With potted orchids, you can estimate how much to water by feeling how damp the compost* is with a touch of your finger, or by holding the pot in your hand to gauge its weight. Keep in mind that smaller pots dry out more quickly than larger ones.

Most experts agree that orchids should be watered in the morning because this gives excess

water the time to trickle out through the other end before the drop in evening temperatures. As in most things, orchid problems are the result of excess. Too much or too little water will lead to the same outcome: leaves wither, turn yellow and fall off, and roots die.

The quality of the water is as important as effective drainage. Rain water at 86° F (30° C) should be used. If this is not possible tap water may be used, provided it is not too soft or too hard. If you have hard water, try softening it with a couple of drops of vinegar. Better yet, use bottled water, but make sure its mineral content is not too high.

Miltonia, Oncidium and some other orchids will let you know if they are being improperly watered by producing wrinkled leaves. Periodic heavy watering can be useful to wash out mineral deposits which lead to root burn. But never let your pots sit in water. Pour the water off, or set the pot on a layer of pebbles. ML

Incorrect watering: the pot should not come into direct contact with the water

Correct watering: clay pebbles keep the pot above the water level

ORCHID SOCIETIES AND ASSOCIATIONS

American Orchid Society
16700 AOS Lane
Delray Beach, FL 33446
Tel: 561404–2000

North of England Orchid Society
130, Regent Rd., Lostock
Bolton BL6 4DE
Tel: 01204 492971

Orchid Society of Great Britain
Athelney, 145 Binscombe Village
Godalming, Surrey GU7 3QL
Tel: 01483 421423

Orchid Society of South East Asia
Robinson Rd,
PO Box 2363
Singapore 904363
Fax: 65–1679677

Orchid Club of South Australia
PO Box 730 GPO
Adelaide SA 5001
(08) 287-1846

S.F.O. Société Française d'Orchidophilie
17-19 quai de la Seine, 75019 Paris
Tel: 01 40 37 36 46

ORCHID NURSERIES AND DISTRIBUTORS

Australasia:

Adelaide Orchids
16 Pine Rd.
Woodcroft SA 5162
Tel: (08) 8381 2011

Atlantis Orchids
Lot 2 Brumbys Rd.
Warrandyte South VIC 3134
Tel: (03) 9844 2826

Burbank Orchids
1330 Mt Gravatt-Capalaba Rd
Burbank QLD 4156
Tel: (07) 3849 8277

Orchids Australia
702 Old Northern Rd.
Dural NSW 2158
Tel: (02) 9651 1294

Orchids Florist
1 O'Connell St.
Sydney NSW 2000
Tel: (02) 9251 5258

Mandai Orchids Garden
Mandai Lake Rd.
Singapore 729827
Tel: 65–2691036
Fax: 65–3361918

The Botanic Garden Shop
Singapore Botanic Garden
1 Cluny Rd.
Singapore 259569
Tel: 65–4636571
Fax: 65–4636572

USA:

A A A Hawaiian Orchids
233 Church St.
Mount Clemens, MI 48043
Tel: (810) 954-3755

A & P Orchids
Swansea, MA 02777
Tel: (508) 675-1717

Baldan Orchids
20075 Sw 180th Ave.
Miami, FL 33187
Tel: (305) 232-8694

Baker & Chantry Orchids
18611 132nd Ave Ne.
Woodinville, WA 98072
Tel: (425) 483-0345

Bakkehelle Orchids
Po Box 1413
Carmel Valley, CA 93924
Tel: (831) 659-1849

Baldan Orchids
20075 Sw 180th Ave.
Miami, FL 33187
Tel: (305) 232-8694

Hanes Orchids Of Distinction
6264 Bion Ave.
San Gabriel, CA 91775
Tel: (626) 287-6474

Pacific Paradise Orchids
Pahoa, HI 96778
Tel: (808) 965-9299

P C Orchids Incorporated
1 Oak Hill Rd.
Fitchburg, MA
01420
Tel: (978) 534-7950

P R A Orchids
3147 Custer Ave.
Lake Worth, FL 33467
Tel: (561) 439-3154

**Pacific Rim Flowers &
Orchid Farm**
6680 Black Rail Rd.
Carlsbad, CA 92009
Tel: (760) 438-2969

Palmer Orchids
1308 Broadway Ave.
Pasadena, TX 77506
Tel: (713) 472-1364

Parkside Orchid Nursery
2503 Mountain View Dr.
Ottsville, PA 18942
Tel: (610) 847-8039

Brazil:

Equilab
P.O. Box 132
13100 Campinas
Tel: (+192) 41 1899
Fax: (+192) 43 24 14

Santa Isabel Orchids
P.O. Box 25
Santa Isabel SP - CEP 07500
Tel: (+192-11) 472-1210

G U I D E

UK:

Exmoor Orchids
The Vandas, Sidbury
Bridgnorth, Salop WV16 6PY

McBeans Orchids Ltd
Coocksbridge, Lewes
East Sussex BN8 4PR
Tel: 01273 400228

Orchids Bagworth
50 Henry Street
Kenilworth, Warwickshire
CV8

Cheshire Orchids
7 Cornwall Close,
Mossley, Congleton,
Cheshire CW12 3JZ
Tel: 01260 270562

Kilgetty Orchids
Moory Park, Jeffreston
Kilgetty Dyfed SA6 8ORT
Tel: 01646 651708

Orchid by Post
Yapton Lane, Walberton
Arundel, West Sussex
BN18 OAS
Tel: 01243 551691

Just Orchids
Brookside Nursery
Church Road, Swallowfield
Reading, Berkshire
RG71TH
Tel: 0118 9886481

Lawrence Hobbs Orchids
Bailiffs Cottage
Hophurst Lane
Crawley, West Sussex
RH10 4LN
Tel: 01342 715142

Deva Orchids
Littlebrook Farm
Stryt Isa, Penyfford
Cheshire, CH4 OJY
Tel: 01978 762454

France:

**Établissements Marcel
Lecoufle / Geneviève Bert**
5, rue de Paris
94470 Boissy-Saint-Léger
Tel: 01 45 6 9 12 79

**Établissements P.F.F.
Vacherot et Lecoufle -
La Tuilerie**
29, rue de Valenton BP 8
94471 Boissy-Saint-Léger cedex
Tel: 01 45 69 10 42

**Exofleur Alfred et Béatrice
Pasenau**
Chemin de Faudouas
31700 Toulouse-Cornebarrieu
Tel: 01 61 85 27 25

**Les Orchidées de Michel
Vacherot**
La Baume D.7
83520 Roquebrune-sur-Argens
Tel: 01 94 45 48 59

Netherlands:

Orchideeën Wubben
Tolakkerweg 162
3739 JT - Hollandsche Rading-
Maartensdijk
Tel: 035 577 1222

Orchideeëncentrum De Wilg
Bermweg 16B
2911 CA - Nieuwerkerk aan
der Yssel
Tel: 018 031 4568

Paul Orchideeën
Oosteinderweg 129B
1432 AH - Aalsmeer
Tel: 029 772 7006

Germany:

Orchideeën von Kühn
Forstweg 12
D - 66132 Saarbrücken
Tel: 0681 89 20 43

Wilhelm Hennis Orchideen
Gr. Venedig 4
D 31134 Hildesheim
Tel: 0512 13 56 77

Wichmann Orchideen
D 29229 Celle
Tel: 0514 13 85 01

Belgium:

Akerne Orchids
Laarsebeekdreef 4
B- 2120 Schoten

S E L E C T E D   B I B L I O G R A P H Y

Orchids and Artists: Five Centuries of Botanical Illustrations. Northampton: Smith College Museum of Art, 1991.

Allikas, Greg. *Orchids.* San Diego, CA: Thunder Bay Press, 2000.

Appell, Scott. *Orchids.* New York: Friedman and Fairfax, 2000.

Berliocchi, Luigi. *The Orchid in Lore and Legend.* Portland, OR: Timber Press, 2000.

Cribb, Phillip. *Orchids: A Romantic History with a Guide to Cultivation.* Philadephia: Running Press, 1992.

Hansen, Eric. *Orchid Fever: A Horticultural Tale of Love, Lust, and Lunacy.* New York: Pantheon Books, 2000.

Kalman, Bela. *Rare Orchids.* Boston, MA: Little, Brown, 1999.

Koopowitz, Harold. *Orchids and their Conservation.* Portland, OR: Timber Press, 2001.

Pridgeon, Alec. *An Illustrated Encyclopedia of Orchids.* Portland, OR: Timber Press, 1992.

Rittershausen, Brian. *Orchids: A Care Manual.* San Diego, CA: Laurel Glen, 2000.

--*Orchids: A Splendid Obsession.* San Francisco: Soma Books, 1999.

Starosta, Paul. *Orchids.* Cologne: Evergreen Press, 1997.

INDEX

INDEX

Photographic credits: Janine Bournerais 86; Yves Delange 54, 55 top left, 100; Jean-Claude Gachet 1, 16–17, 19, 43 bottom, 43 top, 52, 63 top, 66 top left, 66 top right, 66 bottom, 67, 68, 69, 70, 81, 92, 96–97, 100, 104–105; Marcel Lecoufle 42, 45 right, 51 top, 51 bottom, 55 top right, 62 top, 72–73, 78, 87, 94, 112–113; Jean-Pierre Lepabic 15, 21, 26, 38–39 top, 46–47, 53, 59, 60–61, 77, 88–89, 90–91, 92; BERLIN, Bildarchiv Preussischer Kulturbesitz 64–65; GRASSE, Musée International de la Perfumerie 110; LONDON, The Bridgeman Art Library 12–13, 14, 45, 106–107; P. Ferret 114–115, 82–83, 84 top; 76; P. Fernandes 115 top right, 115 bottom right, 45 left, 45 middle, 84 left, 84 right, 84 middle, 94 bottom, 95; PARIS, Bibliothèque centrale du Muséum national d'histoire naturelle 18, 101, 35 bottom, 62–63, 48, 29, 76; Bios 22–23; M. DeprazWWF 40; F. Rouquette 56–57, 102–103; Dagli Orti 41, 50; Jacana; G. Leroy-Terquem 44–45; M. Claye 79; F. Depalle 93; C. Nardin 85 bottom; M. C. Noailles 85 top; Magnum; S. Salgado 32–33; Réunion des musées nationaux 10, 27, 28, 98–99, 42, 74; Roger-Viollet 24–25; Sygma 39 bottom; VANVES, Explorer 111; L. Girard 34 ; J. L. Gobert 108–109.
© ADAGP 1996 for Jacques-Émile Blanche

Translated and adapted from the French by Chet Wiener and Stacey Doris
Copy-editing: Kathryn Lancaster
Typesetting: Muriel Lefebvre
Color separation: Pollina S.A., France

Originally published as *L'ABCdaire des orchidées* © 1996 Flammarion
English-language edition © 2002 Flammarion

ISBN: 2-0801-0674-0
N° d'édition: FA0674-01-XI
Dépôt légal: 3/2002
Printed and bound by Pollina S.A, France - n° L84966

Pages 4–5: *Encyclia vitellina*, Mexico and Guatemala